The Martian Child

The Martian Child

A Novel About a Single Father Adopting a Son

~~~~~~~~~~~~~~~~~~~~~~~~~~~~~~~~~~~~~~~

(Based on a true story)

David Gerrold

A Tom Doherty Associates Book FORGE New York

THE MARTIAN CHILD

Copyright © 2002 by David Gerrold

This book is printed on acid-free paper.

Book design by Jane Adele Regina

A Forge Book
Published by Tom Doherty Associates, LLC
175 Fifth Avenue
New York, NY 10010

www.tor.com

Forge® is a registered trademark of Tom Doherty Associates, LLC.

Library of Congress Cataloging-in-Publication Data

Gerrold, David.
    The Martian child : a novel about a single father adopting a son / David Gerrold.—1st. ed.
        p. cm.
    "Based on a true story."
    ISBN 0-765-30311-6 (alk. paper)
        1. Adopted children—Fiction. 2. Fathers and sons—Fiction.
    3. Abused children—Fiction. 4. Single fathers—Fiction.
    5. Gay fathers—Fiction. 6. Boys—Fiction. I. Title.

PS3557.E69 M35 2002
813'.54—dc21

                                                    2001058285

First Edition: June 2002

Printed in the United States of America

0 9 8 7 6 5 4 3 2 1

For my son, Sean, with love

A novelette version of *The Martian Child* was first published in the September 1994 issue of *The Magazine of Fantasy & Science Fiction*.

In 1995, the novelette version of *The Martian Child* won the Hugo Award, the Nebula Award, and the Locus Readership Poll for best novelette of 1994.

The Martian Child

~~~~~~

Toward the end of the meeting, the caseworker remarked, "Oh—and one more thing. Dennis thinks he's a Martian."

"I beg your pardon?" I wasn't certain I had heard her correctly. I had papers scattered all over the meeting room table—thick piles of stapled incident reports, manila-foldered psychiatric evaluations, Xeroxed clinical diagnoses, scribbled caseworker histories, typed abuse reports, bound trial transcripts, and my own crabbed notes as well: Hyperactivity. Fetal Alcohol Syndrome. Emotional Abuse. Physical

Abuse. Conners Rating Scale. Apgars. I had no idea there was so much to know about children. For a moment, I was actually looking for the folder labeled *Martian*.

"He thinks he's a Martian," Ms. Bright repeated. She was a small woman, very proper and polite. "He told his group home parents that he's not like the other children—he's from Mars—so he shouldn't be expected to act like an Earthling all the time."

"Well, that's okay," I said, a little too quickly. "Some of my best friends are Martians. He'll fit right in. As long as he doesn't bring home any giant alien slugs from outer space."

By the narrow expressions on their faces, I could tell that the caseworkers weren't amused. For a moment, my heart sank. Maybe I'd said the wrong thing. Maybe I was being too glib with my answers.

The hardest thing about adoption is that *you have to ask someone to trust you with a child.*

That means that you have to be willing to let them scrutinize your entire life, everything: your financial standing, your medical history, your home and your belongings, your upbringing, your personality, your motivations, your arrest record, your IQ—even your sex life. It means that *every* self-esteem issue you have ever had will come bubbling right to the surface like last night's beans in this morning's bathtub. And that means—whatever you're most insecure about, that's what the whole adoption process will feel like it's focused on.

The big surprise for me was discovering that what I

thought would be the biggest hurdle was not. Any concerns I might have had about sexual orientation disappeared at a conveniently timed set of seminars on legal issues, held by the Gay-Lesbian Community Center in Hollywood. Two female lawyers, very thorough in their presentations, addressed adoption and custody issues.

"Just tell the truth," they said. "If you lie about who you are, the caseworkers will find out—and then they're going to wonder why you're lying, and what else you might be lying about. And you won't be approved.

"It has taken many years and a lot of hard work by a lot of people to educate caseworkers and judges. There are now six thousand adoptions a year by gay people, mostly in major urban areas. If you are committed and qualified in every other respect, you have the same opportunity as anyone else." And that was all I'd needed to know. After that, it wasn't an issue.

No—what unnerved me the most was that terrible, familiar feeling of being *second* best, of not being good enough to play with the big kids, or get the job, or win the award, or whatever was at stake. So even though the point of this interview was simply to see if Dennis and I would be a good match, I felt as if I was being judged again. What if I wasn't good enough this time either?

I tried again. I began slowly. "Y'know, you all keep telling me all the bad news—you don't even know if this kid is capable of forming a deep attachment—it feels as if you're trying to talk me out of this match." I stopped myself before I said too much. I was suddenly angry and I didn't know why. These people were only doing their job.

And then it hit me. That was it—these people were *only* doing their job.

At that moment, I realized that there wasn't anyone in the room who had the kind of commitment to Dennis that I did, and I hadn't even met him yet. To them, he was only another case to handle. To me, he was . . . a kid who wanted a dad. He was the possibility of a family. It wasn't fair to unload my frustration on this committee of tired, overworked, underpaid women. They cared. It just wasn't the same kind of caring. I swallowed hard—and swallowed my anger.

"Listen," I said, sitting forward, placing my hands calmly and deliberately on the table. "After everything this poor little guy has been through, if he wants to think he's a Martian, I'm not going to argue with him. Actually, I think it's charming. This kid is alone in the world; he's got to be feeling it. At least, this gives him some kind of a handle on it—the only one he's got. It would be stupid to try to take it away from him."

For the first time I looked directly into their eyes as if they had to live up to *my* standards. "Excuse me for being presumptuous—but he's got to be with someone who'll tell him that it's all right to be a Martian. Let the little guy be a Martian for as long as he needs."

"Yes. Thank you," the supervisor said abruptly. "I think that's everything we need to cover. We'll be getting back to you shortly."

My heart sank at her words. She hadn't acknowledged a

word of what I'd said. I was certain she'd dismissed it totally. I gathered up all my papers. We exchanged pleasantries and handshakes and I wore my company smile all the way to the elevator. I didn't say a word, and neither did my sister. We waited until we were in the car and headed back toward the Hollywood Freeway. She drove. She sold real estate; she was in her car all day long. Maybe she could deal with surly traffic; I couldn't. Driving wasn't fun when there were too many other cars on the road.

"I blew it," I said. "Didn't I? I got too . . . full of myself again."

"Honey, I think you were fine." She patted my hand.

"They're not going to make the match," I said. "It would be a single-parent adoption. They're not going to do it. First they choose married couples, Ward and June. Then they choose single women, Murphy Brown. Then, only if there's no one else who'll take the kid, will they consider a single man. I'm at the bottom of the list. I'll never get this kid. I'll never get *any* kid. My own caseworker told me not to get my hopes up. His caseworker says there are two other families interested. Who knows what their caseworkers are telling them? This was just a formality, this interview. I know it. Just so they could prove they'd considered more than one match." I felt the frustration building up inside my chest like a balloon full of hurt. "But this is the kid for me, Alice, I know it. I don't know how I know it, but I do."

I'd first seen Dennis's picture three weeks earlier; a little square of colors that suggested a smile in flight.

I'd gone to the National Conference of the Adoptive Families of America at the Los Angeles Airport Hilton. There were six panels per hour, six hours a day, two days, Saturday and Sunday. I picked the panels that I thought would be most useful to me in finding and raising a child and ordered tapes—over two dozen—of the sessions I couldn't attend in person. I'd had no idea there were so many different issues to be dealt with in adoptions. I soaked it up like a sponge, listening eagerly to the advice of adoptive parents, their grown children, clinical psychologists, advocates, social workers, and adoption resource professionals.

But my *real* reason for attending was to find *the child*.

I'd already been approved. I'd spent more than a year filling out forms and submitting to interviews. But approval doesn't mean you get a child. It only means that your name is in the hat. Matching is done to meet the child's needs first. Fair enough—but terribly frustrating.

Eventually, I ended up in the conference's equivalent of a dealer's room. Rows of tables and heart-tugging displays. Books of all kinds for sale. Organizations. Agencies. Children in Eastern Europe. Children in Latin America. Asian children. Children with special needs. Photo-listings, like real estate albums. Turn the pages, look at the eyes, the smiles, the needs. *Johnny was abandoned by his mother at age three. He is hyperactive, starts fires, and has been cruel to small animals. He will need extensive therapy. . . . Janie, age nine, is severely retarded. She was sexually abused by her stepfather; she will need round-the-clock care. . . . Michael suffers from severe epilepsy. . . . Linda* needs . . . *Danny* needs . . . *Michael* needs . . . So many *needs*. It was overwhelming. How do you even begin to figure who a kid might be from this kind of description?

And why were so many of the children in the books "special needs" children? Retarded. Hyperactive. Abused. Had they been abandoned because they weren't perfect, or were these the leftovers after all the good children were selected? The part that disturbed me the most was that I could understand the emotions involved. I wanted a child, not a case. And some of the descriptions in the book did seem pretty intimidating. Were these the only kind of children available?

Maybe it was selfish, but I found myself turning the pages looking for a child who represented an easy answer. Did I really want another set of *needs* in my life—a single man who's old enough to be considered middle-aged and ought to be thinking seriously about retirement plans?

This was the most important question of all. "Why do you want to adopt a child?" And it was a question I couldn't answer. I couldn't find the words. It was something I couldn't write down.

The motivational questionnaire had been a brick wall that sat on my desk for a week. It took me thirty pages of single-spaced printout just to get my thoughts organized. I could tell great stories about what I thought a family should be, but I couldn't really answer the question why *I* wanted a son. Not right away.

The three o'clock in the morning truth of it was a very nasty and selfish piece of business.

I didn't want to die alone. I didn't want to be left unremembered.

All those books and TV scripts . . . they were nothing. They used up trees. They were exercises in excess. They made other people rich. They were useless to me. They filled up shelves. They impressed the impressionable. But they didn't prove me a real person. They didn't validate my life as one worth living.

What I *really* wanted was to make a difference. I wanted someone to know that there was a real person behind all those words. A dad.

I would lay awake, staring into the darkness, trying to imagine it, what it would be like, how I would handle the various situations that might come up, how I would deal with the day-to-day business of daddying. I gamed out scenarios and tried to figure out how to handle difficult situations.

In my mind, I was always kind and generous, compassionate and wise. My fantasy child was innocent and joyous, full of love and wide-eyed wonder, and grateful to be in my home. He was an invisible presence, living inside my soul, defying reality to catch up. I wondered where he was now, and how and when I would finally meet him—and if the reality of parenting would be as wonderful as the dream.

But it was all Fantasyland. The casebooks were proof of that. These children had histories: brutal, tragic, and heart-rending.

I wandered on to the next table. One of the social workers from the Los Angeles County Department of Children's Services had a photo book with her. I introduced myself, told her I'd been approved—but not matched. Could I look through the book? I turned the pages slowly, studying the innocent faces, looking for one who could be my son. All the pictures were of black children, and the County wasn't doing trans-racial adoptions anymore. Too controversial. The black social workers had taken a stand against it—I could see their point—but how many of these children would not find homes now?

Tucked away like an afterthought on the very last page was a photo of the only white child in the book. My glance slid across the picture quickly. I was already starting to close the album—and then as the impact of what I'd seen hit me, I froze in mid-action, almost slamming the book flat again.

The boy was riding a bicycle on a sunny, tree-lined sidewalk; he was caught in the act of shouting or laughing at whoever was holding the camera. His blond hair was wild in the wind of his passage, his eyes shone like stars behind his glasses, his expression was raucous and exuberant.

I couldn't take my eyes off the picture. A cold wave of certainty came rolling up my spine like a blast of fire and ice. It was a feeling of *recognition*. This was *him*—the child who'd taken up permanent residence in my imagination! I could almost hear him yelling, "Hi, Daddy!"

"Tell me about this child," I said, a little too quickly. The social worker was looking at me oddly. I could understand it;

my voice sounded odd to me too. I tried to explain. "Tell me something. Do you ever get people looking at a picture and telling you that this is the one?"

"All the time," she replied. Her face softened into an understanding smile.

His name was Dennis. He'd just turned eight. She'd just put his picture in the book this morning. So, no, she didn't have much information about him. And yes, she'd have the boy's caseworker get in touch with my caseworker. "But," she cautioned, "remember that there might be other families interested too. And remember, the department always matches from the child's side."

I didn't hear any of that. I heard the words, but not the cautions.

Because I *knew*.

I called Verona, my caseworker, an earth-motherly black woman, and told her that this was the one. I called *his* caseworker and told her that I had to meet this boy. Because I had this *feeling*.

So they set up a meeting to tell me about him—all the stuff I needed to know. Verona told me to bring a family member—my sister—and she cautioned me ahead of time: "This might not be the child you're looking for. He's hyperactive and he has other problems as well, so you don't want to get your hopes up yet."

Hyperactive.

I knew the word, but I didn't really know what it meant. Calvin and Hobbes. Dennis the Menace. Attila the Hun.

Stuff like that. All the stereotypes. A kid who fidgets and squirms, who can't sit still, can't concentrate, can't finish things, can't be controlled. No, I definitely did not want a hyperactive kid with emotional problems, but—

I couldn't shake the *feeling*.

The thing about writing books, you learn how to look things up.

So I posted messages all over CompuServe asking for information and advice on adoption, on attention deficit hyperactivity disorder, on emotional abuse recovery, on behavioral issues, on everything I could think of—what were this child's chances of becoming an independent adult? I called the Adoption Warm Line and was referred to parents who'd been through it. One woman had raised three hyperactive kids; she made it sound like a war zone. One doctor was downright pessimistic. It made me angry. These people didn't even know this little boy.

I hit the bookstores and the libraries. I refused to accept the bad news. I hadn't signed on for failure. I called cousin Ken, the doctor, and he faxed me twenty pages of reports on attention deficit disorder. And I came into the meeting so well-papered and so full of theories and good intentions that I must have looked the perfect jerk.

Verona sat on one side of me; my sister sat on the other side. Emotional bookends. At the head of the table was a supervisor and a couple of her aides, all women. At the other end of the table was Dennis's caseworker, Kathy Bright. After a brief exchange of pleasantries, she opened her folder.

"This picture was taken last month, when he turned eight. The bicycle was his present. That was his one big wish. We didn't really have it in the budget, but he needed it."

She turned the page.

"Dennis's mother was a substance abuser and an alcoholic; she abandoned him in a motel at the age of one and a half. His father died of a self-induced overdose. Dennis has been in eight foster homes in eight years."

I reacted sharply to that. "*What?* Why has he been in the system for so long?"

She ignored the implied accusation. "It took a while to have his mother's parental rights terminated. There were legal issues." She explained: "He was abused in two of his placements. In the first one, the abuse happened between the ages of two and four, so we're not exactly sure what happened; he wasn't able to tell us clearly. He had to testify against the woman. That was very hard for him, and it delayed his availability for adoption.

"And then we had trouble finding a suitable foster home, because he acted out. We had to remove him from his next placement because they were beating him with a belt. That happened when he was five.

"Dennis is hyperactive," she continued. "Attention deficit hyperactivity disorder. He's on Ritalin for the hyperactivity—and Clonodine to counteract the side effects of the Ritalin; the Ritalin gives him muscle tics. We also had him tested for fetal alcohol effects. The results were inconclusive. Here's a copy of the doctor's evaluation.

"Dennis sees a psychiatrist once a month to have his prescription renewed. He's been diagnosed as severely emotionally disturbed. We were hoping he would stabilize, and for a while he did seem to improve in the Johnson group home, but as you can see by the incident reports, his behavior has been deteriorating. We're going to have to move him again soon. Probably to a long-term facility. He's classified as 'hard-to-place.'" She finished her report and put her papers down.

Hard to place.

A euphemism for *unadoptable*.

"We don't know if Dennis is capable of forming a lasting attachment. He engages well with adults, but it's shallow. He knows how to work the system—all the children do—but we don't know if he can bond with a parent. He has no real experience living in a family, he doesn't know how to behave, he acts out, he's obstinate-defiant, and he's destructive—are you sure you can deal with him tearing up your house?"

That gave me pause. I'd been remodeling, adding on, fixing up, sanding and painting for almost twenty years. The house was actually beginning to look like a home. I had to wonder, what kind of damage could one little boy do?

The choice she was asking me to consider was my house or my son. Asked that way, it was no contest. This was a little boy who must be so frightened and angry and hurting, it was beyond comprehension. All I could think of was how desperate he must be. What kind of damage might he do? It didn't matter.

Very quietly, Verona put her hand on mine and whispered, "Don't be a rescuer, David. That doesn't serve you, or him."

But how could I *not* be a rescuer? This boy *needed*—

And yes, I'd heard every word they'd said, and even though part of me was horrified, another part was arguing that it couldn't possibly be that bad, and even if it was, I still had this unquenchable belief that enough love could cure anything—I'd gotten that from my grandmother, who had been the most loving person I'd ever known in my life.

All that stuff, all that bad news—it wasn't a reason to quit. It was a reason to *commit*. I couldn't walk away from his *need*.

Anybody else would have said *never mind* and run screaming from the room. I wanted to say it. This was not the child I had imagined. This was outside the lines I had set; but no matter what they said, I still couldn't escape the feeling that this was my son. The boy in the picture had grabbed my heart so completely that I'd suddenly forgotten all my preexisting ideas of what kind of child I wanted.

Then Kathy Bright slid over a foot-high stack of "incident reports." Things that had happened in the group home. I didn't know what to do with all these papers, the crabbed handwriting, all this incriminating detail.

I don't know why I did it. It wasn't something I'd ever seen anyone else do, and I didn't know what I was looking for, but I picked up the stack and flipped through it, riffling the pages like a flip book, skimming through the dates on the upper right corners of the pages. And I noticed something—

"All of these reports are from the same month, September," I said.

Kathy Bright frowned, remembering. "That was when we took him off the Ritalin and put him on Disipramine. That didn't work at all."

And then—again, I don't know why I did it or what I was looking for—I flipped through the stack again, this time skimming the signatures on the bottom left corners of the pages.

"All these reports were written by the same person," I said. I looked up, inquiringly.

"That was a group-home worker who had control issues," Kathy explained. "He was only there for a month. He didn't work out."

"Oh," I said.

For a weird moment, I had a nightmare vision of this poor little boy, buried under a stack of reports and opinions. If somebody wrote the wrong thing, it didn't matter—it still went into the file. Everything went into the file, no matter what. And if nobody ever questioned the validity of all this paper? If they all just accepted it at face value? What if all of this was wrong? And what if this kid was being defined by other people's misjudgments and mistakes?

I put the reports down. I didn't want to read them. I couldn't trust them. "So all of these incident reports, written about a kid on the wrong medication, by a guy with control issues—these really don't reflect who Dennis is, do they?"

No, they admitted. I felt as if I'd won a small victory. For myself and for Dennis.

"What were his Apgars?" I asked, for want of something else to ask—I was desperate for some good news. Apgar numbers were a measure of a child's health at birth and five minutes after.

Kathy shuffled through her papers. "Eight and nine." Those were good.

"And how does he rate on the Conners scale?"

"That's the ADHD rating, isn't it?" She looked confused.

I opened my own notebook and pulled out two different reports and a ratings sheet. "Here, this is what you need to know about attention deficit hyperactivity disorder, and how to gauge it."

"Oh, wait, I have something here. Is this what you're asking about? I'm not sure how to read these numbers—" She passed over more paper. It wasn't good news. Minus two. Dennis was textbook-perfect ADHD.

Part of me wanted to push all the paper aside, thank them for their time, and head for home.

But the other part of me—the part that had fallen in love with a picture—refused to walk away.

"Look," I said. "All this paper, this isn't Dennis. This is all the bad news, all the stuff that didn't work for someone else. And every time something else doesn't work, it goes into one of these reports and it's another little label this boy has to carry around. I don't see Dennis here. I just see a lot of opinions. Informed opinions, yeah, but—" I looked up and down the table. "Where's the *good* news? Are you telling me there isn't any? I can't believe that." I pushed the papers aside. "This doesn't say what he's really like. To you folks, he's just a case. One more in a whole stack of cases. To me, he's a little boy who needs a dad. I have to *meet* him."

I looked around the table. Their expressions were bland and unreadable. This was just another meeting to them, one more in a long string of meetings with prospective parents. This was about process, nothing else—and reaction wasn't part of the process.

The supervisor changed the subject. She asked, "Kathy, what's your relationship with him? Do you like the boy?"

Kathy Bright said calmly, "No, I don't. He kicked me once." Then she added, "But I do care what happens to him." As if that somehow excused not liking him. "He worries about his future. He asked, 'What's going to happen to me?' He told his counselor, 'I don't think God listens to my prayers. I prayed for a dad and nothing happened.'"

And they didn't want me be a rescuer? How could I not be a rescuer?

There was one other surprise.

The supervisor abruptly turned to me and said, "It says here that you're gay. Is that correct?"

"Yes."

"Exclusively gay? Or bisexual?"

I shrugged. "You can say bisexual." If it makes you more comfortable. If it looks better on your report.

Explaining it would take a short novel—or maybe a trilogy.

There was the red-haired young man—Peter Pan in a white Rambler who went back to Neverland much too soon—who showed me that love has nothing to do with lust. And then there was she-who-will-not-be-named who demonstrated even more horrifically that lust has nothing to do with love. There was she who loved gently and she who loved loudly. And there was he who loved and he who didn't. The only thing that all of these situations had in common was that I was there. The only thing proven by this history was that I was an incurable romantic—I had never stopped believing in the *possibility* of love.

She jotted her note, apparently satisfied. And I didn't pursue it. I don't like classifying people by who they fall in love with. That kind of distinction doesn't make sense to me. The only thing that fits in a pigeonhole is a pigeon.

But we weren't quite done with it yet. Kathy Bright said, "Before David meets Dennis, I'll have to explain it to Dennis."

Before I could open my mouth, my sister spoke up. She said—in that tone of voice that she reserved only for stopping train wrecks before they happen—"*No.*"

Everyone looked to her.

"That will be my brother's responsibility. He'll choose the appropriate time and place." She left no room for discussion, let alone argument. "It isn't a conversation that anyone else should have with the boy. It's David's job to tell him, and it has to be done after they've met, not before. Otherwise, you're influencing the situation unfairly."

Kathy looked like she wanted to object, but the supervisor spoke first. "It's not an issue. Let's move on."

And then Kathy Bright said that thing about Dennis being a Martian and I went off to Fantasyland, relieved to be talking about something else for a minute. At least, I knew fantasy. I was an expert in that.

And then . . . it was over.

I'd made my case. And all I could think of was all the stuff I should have said *instead*. Instead of trying to be so smart.

I leaned my head against the passenger side window of my sister's car and moaned. "Dammit. I'm so *tired* of being pregnant. Thirteen months is long enough for any man! I've got the baby blues so bad, I can't even go to the supermarket anymore. I find myself watching other people with their children and the tears start welling up in my eyes. I keep thinking, 'Where's *mine*?' "

My sister understood. She had four children of her own, none of whom had ended up in jail; so she had to have done something right. "Listen to me, David. Maybe this little boy isn't the right one for you—"

"Of course he's right for me. He's a Martian."

Alice ignored the interruption. "And if he isn't right, there'll be another child who is. I promise you. And you said it yourself that you didn't know if you could handle all the problems he'd be bringing with him."

I'd admitted it to her, no one else. It was the first time in my life I'd ever doubted my ability to do something. "It's just that I feel like . . . I don't know what I feel like. This is worse than anything I've ever been through. All this wanting and not having. Sometimes I'm afraid it's not going to happen at all."

Alice pulled the car over to the curb and turned off the engine. "Okay, it's my turn," she said. "Stop beating yourself up. You are the smartest one in the whole family, but sometimes you can be awfully stupid. You are going to be a terrific father to some very lucky little boy. Your caseworker knows that. All of those social workers in that meeting saw your commitment and dedication. All that research you did—when you asked about the Apgar numbers and the Conners scale, when you handed them that report on hyperactivity, which even they didn't know about—you *impressed* them."

I shook my head. "Research is easy. You post a note on CompuServe, wait two days, and then download your e-mail."

"It's not the research," Alice said. "It's the fact that you did it. That demonstrates your willingness to find out what the child needs so you can provide it."

"I wish I could believe you," I said.

She looked at me. "What's the matter?"

"What if I'm really *not* good enough?" I said. "*That's* what I'm worried about—I can't shake that feeling."

"Oh, that—that's *normal.*"

"That's what it feels like to be a parent?"

She nodded. "That—and the lack of sleep. When Jon was

born, when we were leaving the hospital, I said to the doctor, 'You're sending this baby home with two people who've never taken care of a baby before.' And he said, 'I do it almost every day. And it still scares the hell out of me.'

"I'll bet that's what those caseworkers are feeling right now—panic. Even worse than you. Because they *need* to find a home for this little boy. There's so much at stake here for this little boy. It's a big risk. You heard what they said about adoptions that fail. It hurts the parents as much as the kids. So, you're right to be scared. Maybe the time to worry is when you're *not*."

She hugged me. "You'll do fine. Now let's go home and call Mom before she busts a kidney from the suspense."

Two centuries later, although the calendar insisted otherwise, Ms. Bright called me. "We've made a decision. If you're still interested in Dennis, we'd like to arrange a meeting."

I don't remember a lot of what she said after that; most of it was details about how we would proceed, but I do remember what she said at the end. "I want to tell you the two things that helped us make the decision. First, it was very clear to all of us that you're committed to Dennis's well-being. That's very important in any adoption, but especially in this one. The other thing was what you said at the end of the meeting—about understanding his need to be a Martian. We were really touched by your empathy for his situation. We think that's a quality that Dennis is going to need very much in any family he's placed in. That's why we decided to try you first."

I thanked her profusely; at least, I think I did. I was suddenly having trouble seeing. And the box of tissues had gone empty.

~~~~~~~~~~~~~~~~~~~~~~~~~~~~~~

I WAS TO MEET DENNIS THREE DAYS later at the Johnson group home in Culver City, a facility specifically for troubled or abused children. Dennis was one of six children living at the home: four boys, two girls.

Because the caseworkers didn't want him to know that he was being auditioned, the group-home parents would introduce me to him as a friend. I met with them early in the day while all the children were away at school.

Randy was a great, genial bear of a man. He seemed to have an inexhaustible store of patience and goodwill. His wife, Roseanne, was thin and capable, but she looked tired and resigned. They'd been running the group home for four years, and clearly they were both ready for a break.

They told me a little bit about Dennis. He was a picky eater, he made weird noises, he didn't get along with the other kids, he threw toys at the walls. They showed me his room. All the holes in the wall were over the bed of the other boy who shared the room.

Randy said that Dennis would argue with the sunrise. One time the box of Cheerios had a picture of a bowl of cereal and strawberries, so Dennis insisted that there had to be strawberries in the box. Even after they poured out the whole box of Cheerios into a big bowl to show him that there were no strawberries, he was unconvinced. He grew angry and argued that someone must have stolen the strawberries.

Roseanne said Dennis had been in the group home for two years. He'd improved for a while, for the first six months, but now his behavior was declining again, and there was talk of moving him to a permanent institution.

They told me about the other children in the home, José, Naomi, Jaime, Tony, Rosa—each of them with their own histories, each of them a conflicted package of problems and traumas. The other children didn't like Dennis, she said. He was the scapegoat, the one they always blamed for everything. And when he arrived home from school, one or another of the children would always say something like "Oh, *yichh*, Dennis is home." So now Randy always picked Dennis up early, so he was home before any of the others, so he wouldn't have to hear that.

But then Roseanne said the thing that hurt the most. "You're thinking of adopting Dennis?" she asked.

"Yes."

She shook her head. "I wouldn't. I wouldn't adopt him."

So many thoughts went through my head so fast, so many different things *not* to say—

I'm sure I was wearing my polite face. If I wasn't, Roseanne didn't appear to notice. Inside, I was seething. Wasn't there anybody who actually *liked* this boy?

The phone rang. It was the school. Dennis was being suspended (again) for acting out. Would you please come pick him up *now*? Randy excused himself. "This won't take long."

I sat on the couch, sipping iced tea, wondering if Dennis would like me. Always, in my fantasies of parenthood, I'd assumed that he would.

But the child who came home from school was a sullen little zombie. He walked through the living room and passed me with no sign of recognition. He headed straight to his room. I said, "Hi." He grunted something that could have been "h'lo" and kept on going.

I felt cheated. I recognized him. Why hadn't he recognized me? I had to remind myself that *I* was the grown-up here, not him. After a bit, he came out of his room and asked me to play table hockey.

For the first few minutes, he was totally intent on the game. I didn't exist to him. Then I remembered an exercise from one of my communications courses—about simply *being with* another person. I stopped trying so hard to do it *right*, and instead just let it all be just the way it already was.

And yet, I couldn't turn off the analytical part of my mind. After reading all those reports, and hearing the opinions of the caseworkers, I couldn't help but watch for evidence. I couldn't see it. None of it. All I could see was a child.

Then that *thing* happened that always happens to any adult who is willing to play with a child. I rediscovered my own childhood. I got involved in the game, and very shortly I was *having fun*, smiling and laughing with him, returning the same delight and approval at every audacious play.

And that's how it started. He began to realize that there was a real human being on the opposite side of the game board. Something sparked. He started reacting to me instead of to the puck. I could feel the sense of connection almost as a physical presence.

He won the first round, I won the second, then he won the third round and exulted. His eyes were bright and his smile was so happy, you could drown in it.

Then, abruptly, Randy said that it was time for Dennis to do his chores. So we loaded up the little red wagon with all the aluminum cans from the little recycling bin and walked them over to the big recycling bin at the nearby park. On the way, we talked. He talked, I listened. "This is where I fell off my bike and needed a stitch in my chin, see?" "Over there is where my friend, John, used to live, but he moved away." "I played soccer last year. I got a trophy."

On the way back, he insisted that I pull the wagon so he could ride in it. By now, he was glowing. He was the boy in the photograph.

When we got back to the group home, the other children had returned from school and were playing loudly in the driveway. Exuberant yard hockey. They looked like normal kids, all of them.

A little Latino girl, maybe five years old, came running up to ask, "Is this your new friend, Dennis?" Without answering, he broke away from me and ran up the driveway, all the way to the back of the yard and into the open garage where he flung himself facedown into the corner of a large old couch. He was suddenly as apart from the other children—indeed the whole world—as it was possible to get.

I walked back into the house and watched him from a rear window. He wasn't crying, but he might as well have been. He wasn't glowing anymore. At that moment, I knew I couldn't leave him. Whatever other problems he might have, my commitment was *bigger*. It had to be.

At Randy's urging, I went outside to join the boys in a game of driveway hockey. I went over to the couch and asked Dennis if he wanted to play. Without acknowledging me, he got up and found a couple of hockey sticks. He handed me one and ran to the game. Whatever bond had existed between us before, he wasn't going to acknowledge it now.

So, I played yard hockey for a while, with a group of boys I didn't know, didn't really want to know—while the boy I wanted to know better kept a calculated distance from me.

After the game, the group-home parents invited me to stay for dinner with the children. I hadn't planned on it, but all the children insisted that I stay, so I did, specifically making a point of sitting next to Dennis. Fried chicken, mashed potatoes, green peas, and eventually ice cream.

Dennis didn't talk at all. He ate quietly and timidly. I tried including him, but without much luck. It was as if he had retreated to a distant moon.

The other children interrogated me mercilessly. Was I married? No. What kind of car did I drive? The white convertible out front. Did I have any children? No, not yet. Did I have a dog? That one, at least, I could answer.

"Yes, I do."

"What's his name?" asked Rosa.

"Somewhere. His name is Somewhere."

"That's a stupid name for a dog."

"No, it isn't. It's a perfect name. You know why? He never gets lost. I always know where he is."

"How?" asked Tony, one of the more excitable children.

"Because he's always Somewhere."

Rosa and Tony shrieked with laughter. José groaned. Dennis didn't say anything.

I turned to Dennis. "Do you know why I named him Somewhere?"

Dennis shook his head.

"Because I read a lot. And sometimes people write stories where they say, 'Somewhere a dog barked.' And I always thought it would be fun to have a dog named Somewhere, so I could say, 'Somewhere, a dog, barked.'"

"Does he bark?" asked Rosa.

"You know what? He doesn't bark at all."

"Never?"

"Never. I have never heard him bark. Do you want to see his picture?" I took out my wallet.

José glowered at me. He was twelve. He knew everything already. He knew I was being silly. He looked at Somewhere's picture and dismissed it with a sniff. "What an ugly dog."

"Hey," I said. "Even ugly dogs need loving—" And as I said it, the resonance of that accidental insight gave me an uncomfortable chill.

Abruptly, Tony piped up. "Do you know what Dennis said?"

Tony was sitting directly across from me. He had that look of malicious mischief common to children who are about to tell a secret and betray a confidence.

"What?" I asked, with queasy foreboding.

"Dennis said he wishes you were his dad." Without looking, I could see that beside me Dennis was already cringing, readying himself for the inevitable, politely worded rejection.

Instead, I turned to Dennis, focusing all my attention on him, and said, "Wow, what a great wish. *Thank you!*"

There was more I wanted to say, but I couldn't. Not yet.

"Better watch out," Tony piped up. "He might make it a Martian wish, and then you'll *have* to."

I didn't understand what Tony meant. It didn't matter. Children say all kinds of things, assuming that adults already understand. I snuck a peek at Dennis. He was staring into his plate. I couldn't tell what he was thinking.

RANDY WALKED ME OUT TO THE CAR.
He walked, I levitated.

"Thanks," I said. "For everything."

"You made quite an impression on him."

"How can you tell? He barely smiled."

"He never took his eyes off you."

I took my car keys out of my pocket, trying to sort it all out, making small talk. "How do you handle all of them?"

"It's a lot of work, but we have assistants." He looked at me. "So, what do you think?"

I didn't have to think, I already knew. "He's wonderful."

"He's a tough kid to handle," he cautioned.

I opened my car door. A thought occurred to me. I stopped and turned back to Randy. "Did you ever watch *Star Trek?*"

"All the time."

"Did you ever think Mr. Spock was a schmuck?"

"Huh?" He looked at me, puzzled.

"All that logic—but no passion. It took me a few years, but I finally figured out why that bothered me so much."

"Why?"

"Because if we let logic rule our lives, we'll never take any chances at all, will we?"

FOR THE NEXT SIX WEEKS, I SAW Dennis twice a week.

On Tuesdays I would drive down to Culver City and we'd walk over to the park. Once we walked over to the mall and I bought him a book and asked him to read it to me. Another time we went out for pizza. Once we drove down to the beach and talked about nothing in particular.

But Saturdays were the good days, the best days. I'd pick him up and bring him back to the San Fernando Valley. I had a 1970 white Cougar convertible, and we'd put the top down and cruise along the freeway. Dennis would sit high in the passenger seat watching the rest of the world with a smile so wide it was life-threatening. If he was as nervous as I was, it didn't show. I just wanted him to have fun—I wanted him to like me.

The first time Dennis walked into the house, something unusual happened.

Somewhere, the dog, *barked*.

I stared at him in surprise. He had the deepest bark I'd ever heard.

The dog was a shaggy black doofus with brown eyebrows

and muttonchops; the perfect pooch for a dog-food ad. Whenever I said, "Let's go to work," wherever he was in the house, Somewhere would pick himself up and laboriously *pad-pad-pad* into my office where he'd squelch himself flat and scrooch his way under the desk, with a great, impassioned Jewish sigh of "I hope you appreciate what I do for you."

He'd stay there all day—as long as the computer was on. Somewhere would only come out for two things: cookies and the doorbell . . . and the doorbell was broken. It had been broken for as long as I'd lived in this house.

Somewhere had just enough intelligence to keep out of the way and more than enough intelligence to find his dinner dish—as long as no one moved it. He spent his mornings resting under my desk, his afternoons snoozing behind the couch, his evenings at the foot of the water bed. He spent the hours before dawn in the dark space underneath the headboard, dreaming about the refrigerator.

Whenever I came home, Somewhere was waiting for me. He had learned to recognize the sound of the car pulling up. He would push the blinds aside with his big, black picklenose and look out the window to make sure, and then he'd wait by the front door. But if anyone else came to the door, Somewhere would back away and cower under a table, even from family or friends or neighbors, folks he'd known for years. The pooch would keep his distance, not comfortable having anyone else on his turf.

But when Dennis came through the door, Somewhere *barked*. Just once. A deep woof of recognition. And then he trotted over to sniff.

Dennis looked wide-eyed at Somewhere and blinked. "That's a big dog." And then, to Somewhere, he said, "Hello."

Something must have connected because Somewhere didn't back away. He wagged his tail three times *and then he let Dennis pat his head*. And in that moment, they were friends. Somewhere, the coward, had made friends with a complete stranger.

Dennis wanted to see the whole house. Somewhere trotted after us from room to room. Dennis politely approved of everything. The kitchen was nice. The TV room was nice. The extra bedroom.

"Whose room is this?" The question was loaded with obvious subtext.

It's yours, I wanted to say. *I spent a month painting and furnishing and decorating it, before I ever knew you. The color of the paint, the shelves, even the books on the shelves, everything was planned for you.*

"It's nobody's. It's for guests. Maybe one weekend you'll stay overnight. You'll sleep in this room. Do you like it?"

"Yes. It's nice."

"Do you want to go swimming now?"

"You have a pool?"

"Uh-huh. I keep it in the backyard. Come on, I'll show you."

The yard was green and flowery, a wall of red and purple and orange bougainvillea surrounded by clusters of gaudy, nameless horrors, selected for no other reason than the brilliance of their colors. In the bright summer light, the backyard sparkled like Munchkinland. The pool was a dark-blue invitation in the center of a riotous jungle.

"It's big."

"Do you want to go swimming?"

"Okay."

But he stopped on the top steps, shivering, and wouldn't come in any further.

He couldn't swim.

"All right, I'll teach you."

"No." He shook his head.

"I won't let you get hurt. It's easy."

"Nuh-uh." He was adamant. He couldn't trust me. Or anyone.

Okay, I wouldn't pressure him.

I'd been there myself, a long long time ago.

Not a problem.

I went to the garage and pulled out a couple of Styrofoam paddleboards. I tossed one in his direction and grabbed the other myself. I dog-paddled around with it for a while, then looked over to him.

"Okay, now, you try."

"Let me use *that* one." He pointed to the board in my hands, even though there was an identical paddleboard floating right next to him. I passed it over.

"Hold onto it with both hands. Kick with your legs and follow me. Bet you can't catch me. Attaboy, that's the way!"

Pretty soon, the frown on his face turned into a smile. After that, everything else was details.

Later, we sat out on the patio and had the most perfect dinner in the world.

I made spaghetti sauce with my own secret recipe: brown some ground beef, cut in some mushrooms and onions, pour a jar of Paul Newman's Industrial Strength Spaghetti Sauce over everything, add a can of diced tomatoes, and a spoonful of grape or strawberry jelly to round off the sharpness of the tomatoes. Boil water. Put butter and salt in the boiling water, then drop in the noodles. Stir the noodles around so they don't stick to each other. After exactly eight and a half minutes, rinse the noodles in hot water so they don't get gummy. Serve with French bread, Parmesan cheese, Caesar salad, and a grin.

Dennis helped. He set the table, he stirred the noodles, he poured the Cokes. I prompted him to say grace. "Thank you, God, for this good food."

I watched him eat with as much pride as if I'd invented the whole idea of food. I was feeling like a Jewish mother. He ate a couple of forkfuls and then he slowed down to a polite nibble. *Was something wrong?*

"Don't you like it?"

Dennis looked across at me. "This is the best spaghetti I ever had."

"Oh, good. I'll give you the recipe."

He put his fork down and pushed the plate away. "Okay, I'm ready for dessert."

"Excuse me? You haven't eaten anything."

"I'm full."

"If you're too full to finish your spaghetti, then you're too full for dessert." That was *my* dad talking. *Hi, Dad.*

Dennis gave me a startled look. He hadn't expected to be challenged.

Slowly, Dennis pulled his plate back and resumed eating.

"Good. Now I don't have to tell you about all the children starving in Albania." *Hey, this parenting business isn't that hard after all, is it?*

This time, he made a noticeable dent in the spaghetti before pushing the plate away. He'd only eaten half of it, but I didn't make an issue of it. I didn't have a lot of experience with child-sized portions. I usually served folks who massed two or three or four times as much as this little creature, so maybe I had given him too much.

Of course, there was that *other* thing to remember. Children have multi-dimensional stomachs, infinitely expandable for things like ice cream, cake, popsicles, cookies, stuff like that—but faced with broccoli, carrots, smashed potatoes, and other things that only a mother would approve, their stomachs shrink to subatomic size. Even looking at a plate of vegetables is enough to trigger an announcement of terminal satiation.

Therefore, no matter how wise the adult, it is impossible to estimate the capacity of any child's stomach. No matter how small the portion you put on the plate, it is always larger than the child's stomach can hold. It remains the most confounding of all topological mysteries.

Never mind that. This wasn't about food. It was about fun. I served dessert. A nice slice of pound cake, fresh whipped cream, plump, juicy strawberries so sweet they glittered. Dennis ate small bites—slowly, carefully—as if trying to make it last.

There were extra strawberries. I reached over and put one on his dessert. Then another. And another. His eyes went *wide*. His expression told the whole story. Nobody had ever done that for him before. In the group home, there are never any extra strawberries. I had to turn away for a minute, to rub my eyes.

~~~~~~~~~~~~~~~~~~~~~~

THE FOLLOWING SATURDAY, I GAVE Dennis fins, a mask, and a snorkel. I showed him how to put them on, then got out of his way.

By the end of the afternoon, he was swimming. He still wouldn't let anyone help him—he had to do it himself—but that was okay. I needed him to be pool safe. I didn't care how he got there.

Later that day, we ran errands. We went to the store to

buy fixings for dinner—more spaghetti. And then Dennis wanted to take Somewhere for a walk. Or maybe it was Somewhere who wanted to take Dennis. He'd never had a boy of his own before and he was very excited about it. Once the leash was on, he dragged Dennis up and down the sidewalk, showing him off to every tree in the neighborhood.

Finally Dennis asked, "How come he has to pee on every tree?"

"Because that's how dogs leave messages for each other."

"No, it isn't—" He gave me a suspicious look.

"Uh-huh. Aren't you glad we have a telephone?"

Dennis considered it. Finally he announced, "You're silly."

"Thank you. That's a compliment. There isn't enough silly in the world. We have to make as much as we can." I turned to him. "Go ahead. Show me your silly face."

Dennis looked puzzled and confused.

"Look, I'll show you. This is a silly face—" I hooked my fingers into the corners of my mouth, I pulled one side up and the other side down, simultaneously crossing my eyes. I had no idea what this face looked like. Mirrors had shattered the last six times. "Now, it's your turn."

Dennis didn't do anything. He just stared at me.

"Aww, come on, Dennis—even the dog can do it. Come here, Somewhere, and show Dennis your silly face."

Somewhere trotted over to me. I leaned down close and blew a puff of air at him, *"Pooh."* Immediately, he flattened himself on the ground and wiped at his face with both paws, as if trying to scrape away something awful. *"Thpfffft!"* I added, and *"Lbrlbrlbrlbr!"* And finally, worst of all, adding insult to injury, *"You are a pickle-nose!"*

That was the last straw. Somewhere *yowped* a whimper of dismay and embarrassment, then scrambled sideways away from me, wiping his face in anguish along the grass, all the while *rumphffling* in surrender. Then abruptly, he bounced back to his feet and shook himself in canine outrage. *"Rowf!"* he protested, which wasn't really a bark, but more of a *rowf*. His tail wagged excitedly. *Let's do that again!*

"There, see? If the dog can make a silly face, so can you."

Dennis thought about it for a moment, then squinched up his face and stuck his tongue out. Not a great silly face, but at least it was a place to start. "I can see we're going to have to practice our silly faces. I think I have an unbroken mirror somewhere."

Dennis didn't have a chance to respond. Somewhere yanked him sideways, and they were off to inspect another tree. Somewhere wanted to check for messages from the mastiff down the street.

We walked around the block to the veterinarian's office. Somewhere needed a booster shot. Dr. Michael Brown had been taking care of my animals for nearly twenty years; by now he was practically family, and Noreda Animal Clinic was the first stop for any new family member, four-legged or otherwise.

After Somewhere had received his booster and a biscuit,

I lifted Dennis up onto the table and said, "Next." Dennis's eyes went wide.

Dr. Brown made a show of looking through Dennis's hair. "I don't see any fleas," he announced. "You can keep him." Automatically, he handed Dennis a dog biscuit. Dennis frowned at it, then passed it on to Somewhere, who was happy to receive a bonus biscuit. He crunched it noisily.

And in that moment, I saw what the future would look like—a father, a son, a dog: a *family.*

A few days later, I dropped by Dr. Brown's office and asked him what he thought of Dennis.

"Good-looking kid."

"Yeah, I think so too."

"What's the problem?"

I did the capsule report. Abandoned by his birth mother, diagnosed with possible fetal-alcohol effects, ritually abused in one foster home, beaten in another, hyperactive, severely emotionally disturbed, mis-medicated, Ritalin (and Clonodine to counteract the side-effects of the Ritalin), scapegoated and teased by the other children in the group home, given to nightmares and muscle tics—

"What's your point?"

"Well . . . I keep asking myself if maybe he isn't too much for me to take on. I'm thinking that maybe I should wait for an easier kid . . ."

Michael Brown, who had known me for twenty years, who had seen me through half a dozen dogs and at least as many cats, raised an eyebrow and looked at me. "David," he said. "That's *not* your style."

And that settled that.

He was right.

In the days that followed, every time I started to run through my doubts again—all the stories, all the opinions, all the case histories in the adoption books—every time I started to fret, I'd hear Michael Brown's simple declaration again. "That's *not* your style."

Hell. I didn't even know I had a style.

~~~~~~~~~~~~~~~~~~~~~~~~~

Six weeks of Saturdays streamed by like a honeymoon. By a not-so-curious coincidence, we always had one or two visitors on Saturday afternoons. One day, it was Roz, our next-door neighbor, who just came by to chat; oh, and who's this, nice to meet you, Dennis. Another day, it was my nephew, Jon, who came to fix the backyard sprinklers, working quietly while I paddled with Dennis. When he finished, he jumped into the pool with us for a game of splash. A third time, it was Verona, who joined us for dinner. No one stayed too long, just long enough to say hello and exchange a knowing smile.

And then—the last week of summer—it was time to try

an overnight visit. We planned it for Saturday. I needed to know what he was like in the morning, how he reacted before he had his first pill of the day, if he was *manageable*. For me, this would be the critical test. Could I deal with him in the morning?

On Thursday, Kathy Bright called.

"Is there a problem?"

"I need to know your intentions regarding Dennis."

I hesitated. "I was planning to wait until October, and then make up my mind—"

"We have to make a decision about his placement."

"Today? But we haven't had our first overnight yet."

"I need to place him before the end of the month."

There was something odd about the way she said it. "Why? What's the rush?"

"We have to move Dennis. The group home is closing next month and we have to find new placements for all the children. Dennis is getting too old for any group-home placement, and there really aren't any that are suitable for a child with his needs. But there's an institution, out of town—"

"No. Don't do that. *I want him.*"

"You're sure?"

The truth? No, I wasn't sure. I'd never be sure. I'd probably spend the rest of my life wondering if I had let my own selfish vanity get in the way of whatever it was I used for logic. But I'd already wrassled this dilemma around the block six times a day ever since she'd pushed that first stack of paper at me. Can I do this? Or will I screw things up so badly that I'll end up adding even more pain to this child's misery? If I adopt him and then I find that I can't handle it—what then? This kid will end up with even more evidence that he can't be loved, can't have a home, can't have a *dad*.

On the other side of that argument, there was me.

For two years now, I'd been researching adoption. I had a shelf full of books and tapes about all kinds of issues—adopting the older child, the sexually abused child, single-parenting, Parent Effectiveness Training, hyperactivity, and a whole slew of other advice books; so many books that if I sat down to read them all, Dennis would be grown before I finished— and so many tapes that I'd have to drive to New York and back six times just to hear them all.

And then there were all those courses.

Ever since Theodore Sturgeon* had dragged me kicking and screaming into the *est* training ten years earlier, I'd been working my way through every personal effectiveness seminar in California. At least, it felt that way. I'd been through the communication workshop, the forum, the advanced

---

*If you were to ask me who I thought were the ten best authors in the field of science fiction, Theodore Sturgeon would be at least three of them. One remarkable evening, he taught me a magical technique of word wizardry that resolved forever the fundamental dilemma of "literary style." Another day, he taught me an even more profound lesson about the nature of humanity. Ted had an unquenchable ability to ask the next question, in life as well as in his work, and every time he did, he would discover and reveal a new facet of humanity as a species capable of profound love. I admired and trusted him enormously. He also had an infinite repertoire of horrendous puns and frightful jokes. I still miss picking up the phone and hearing his lyrical voice on the other end of the line.

course, the leadership course, the breakthrough course, the experience course, and a half dozen more whose names and purposes I couldn't remember anymore—all of them proof how determined I was that no one could ever be more enlightened than me.

All those seminars had to have made some difference. Everything I'd discovered about myself, all the coaching for results, all the training in how to listen to others, how to speak to them—it wasn't supposed to be theory. It was supposed to be *applied to the processes of life.*

And *that* was the realization. *This* was what I'd been training for. *This was it.*

Dennis.

The uncomfortable truth was that there wasn't anyone else on this entire planet who wanted Dennis. Yes, there had been people who were interested—but interest is a long way from commitment. Look how hard it had been for me to get past my own reservations. And if the caseworkers and group-home parents didn't believe in Dennis, why should anyone else? Hell, they'd almost scared *me* off.

I'd never admit it, but I was too prideful to quit. I couldn't imagine anyone else bringing the same kind of determination, making the same kind of effort for this kid. This was the certainty of the moment—there wasn't anybody else as well-trained for this moment as I was. If they gave out college degrees in Dennis, I'd have a Ph.D. The uncomfortable truth was—whether I was ready or not, this was it. If I wasn't ready for him now, I'd never be. *And neither would anybody else.*

I was his best chance.

And how could I let him go now? After all that time we'd spent together. It wouldn't be fair to just stop seeing him. I couldn't hurt him like that—leaving him wondering, "What's wrong with me that David stopped coming?"

And after I finished walking through all those painful thoughts, I was left with the only one that mattered.

I loved him.

I'd already been showing his picture around for six weeks, bragging to all of my friends and colleagues, "This is the kid I'm adopting. This little boy is going to be my son."

So why was I hesitating?

Because. *This was it.*

"Yes," I finally said. "Let's do it. I want him."

Kathy Bright was curiously detached. All business. "Do you want me to tell him?"

"No, I should do it."

Already I was thinking like a dad. Kids in the foster care system—all their lives, other people make decisions for them about where they're going to live and who they're going to live with. Their lives are out of their control. What kind of frustration and helplessness must these kids feel?

"It has to be his decision too. Let me ask him what he wants to do this weekend."

Family building has to be a choice. The commitment has to come from both sides. Otherwise, it's just another placement, just another place to live. I didn't want to do more of the same. I wanted this to be special. Dennis had to have his own opportunity to choose. And I wanted Dennis to want me as much as I wanted him.

Saturday afternoon, I decided to drop the first pebble in the water, to see how he would react. We were driving to the beach, and I was silently rehearsing what to say next. I chose my first words carefully. "You know, we have so much fun together, I wish you could stay with me all the time."

Dennis replied, so soft I almost missed it. "You could adopt me."

My heart nearly stopped.

I shouldn't have been surprised. At one of the seminars, the adoption expert had said that the children are intuitive. They know what's going on. They know how the system works.

Dennis was waiting for my response. I answered gently, "That's a good idea. Yeah, I could do that."

Before I could say anything else, Dennis began to explain the whole process to me. I had to wonder how long he'd been thinking about it—probably since the very first day, since the moment he'd first whispered his secret to Tony. He said, "You have to call Kathy, my caseworker, and ask her if you can adopt me. And if she says it's all right, then I come and live with you. And then she comes to check on me every month to make sure you're treating me nice and not hitting me or anything."

"Oh," I said. I decided to follow his lead. "Is that how it works?"

"Uh-huh." He was very earnest. He'd made his case. Now it was up to me.

"Is that what you want to do?"

"Yes."

"Me too—let's do it."

It hadn't been the conversation I had so carefully planned, but so what—this was even better. I pulled out my cell phone and flipped it open like Captain Kirk. Dennis's eyes went wide as I dialed Kathy's number. By now, I had it memorized.

"Hello, Kathy? Yes, it's David. I'm here with Dennis. He's right here beside me. We've just had a very interesting conversation. I told him that I like him so much that I wish he could live with me, and he suggested that I adopt him. But I have to ask your permission. So I'm calling to ask if I can adopt Dennis."

"That's the way he explained it to you?"

"Yes. He was very definite."

"All right, let's do it his way. Let me speak to him."

I passed the phone over to him. "Here, Kathy wants to talk to you."

He took the phone and held it up to his ear tentatively. He'd never spoken on a cell phone before. "Hello?" I watched his face. "Uh-huh . . . uh-huh . . . uh-huh . . . uh-huh . . . uh-huh." He closed up the cell phone and handed it back to me.

"What did she say?"

He answered very calmly, "She said yes."

Whew.

"All right, then it's settled. I'm going to adopt you. You're going to be my son. And I'm going to be your dad. *Wow!* Look at you—that is the best happy face I've ever seen! I want you to wear that face tonight. We're going to have dinner at Grandma's and she's going to want to see a happy face."

He thought about that for a minute. "I'm going to have a Grandma and a Grandpa?"

"The best Grandma and Grandpa in the world. You'll meet them tonight. Grandma Jo and Grandpa Harvey. They're going to love you so much."

"Will I have any aunts and uncles?"

"You'll have Aunt Alice, she's my sister. And you'll have Uncle Jimmy and Aunt Betty. Jimmy's my stepbrother."

"Will I have any cousins?"

"Oh, you'll have lots and lots of cousins. Our family makes cousins like other families make cupcakes. You already met Jon—he'll be your cousin. And Mollie and Matt and Cindy and Rachel and Mae Beth. And if that's not enough, we'll make more. Mollie is getting married in December, so you'll get another cousin there."

"Will there be a wedding?"

"Uh-huh."

"I should get to go to the wedding," he said, very carefully arguing his case for inclusion. "If I'm going to be in the

family, I should get to go all the family things." I wondered at
his phrasing, the unspoken assumption that he had to argue
for acceptance, that others had excluded him in the past.

"Well," I said, "we do need a ring bearer for the
wedding . . ."

"A ring bearer? What's that?"

I held up my hand just about his height. "That's a little
guy about so tall who carries the wedding rings down the aisle
on a little pillow."

"Oh!" shouted Dennis, focusing on the level of my hand.
"That's a midget!" And then, excitedly: "You don't have to
hire a midget! I can do it!"

"Sure, why not. Aunt Alice will be thrilled. Midgets are
expensive."

I whipped out the cell phone again. She wasn't there, but
we left a message. "Your new nephew has something to tell
you." I handed him the phone.

"You don't have to hire a midget," he insisted to the
phone. "I can be the ring bearer at the wedding."

I had to smile, thinking of her reaction to that message. It
wouldn't be any stranger than any of the other messages I'd
left on her answering machine over the years, like "Mr. Spock
needs a real estate agent." Or "Have you got any haunted
houses?"

We arrived at the beach, and walked around for a while,
looking at the water and talking about our family contract. I
had a pad of paper and I made careful notes.

"You tell me what you think a dad should do," I said. He

thought about it for a moment. "Be nice" was at the top of the list. "And don't hit."

"That sounds good to me. How about this one? 'Always love you.'"

He nodded. "Okay."

"And in return . . . you have to tell the truth. No lying, okay?"

"Okay."

I wrote it all down, and then we both signed it. And that was that.

Just one more thing.

That *other* conversation.

I waited a while longer. Working up my courage. Telling my mom hadn't been as tough as this.

"Dennis?"

"Yeah?"

"I have to talk to you about something else."

He gave me his most serious-listening look.

"Do you know what it means when someone is gay?"

He nodded.

"What?"

"It means they're happy."

"Well, yes—it does. But it also means something else. I'm gay. That means—well, some boys would rather have boyfriends than girlfriends. And some girls would rather have girlfriends than boyfriends. Do you understand that?"

He considered it. "Uh-huh."

"You're sure?"

He studied me carefully, as if trying to figure it out. "You'd rather have a boyfriend?"

"Uh-huh."

"So I'm not going to have a mom?"

"No. You're not going to have a mom. It's going to be just you and me."

For a moment, I doubted myself—was this fair to Dennis? Telling him like this? But how else—*when* else—could I have told him? But for a moment, all I could hear were all the critics in the world condemning me for offering this little boy a dad, and then, only after he said yes, telling him that Dad was—

Dad was fine. Dad didn't listen to other people's opinions about his capacity for love. That way lies madness. I just needed to make sure that it wasn't a problem for Dennis.

"Listen, it doesn't change anything, sweetheart. I love you and I want you to be my son. And I want you to know who I am, because I don't want us to have any secrets. Remember what we promised—no lying?"

"Uh-huh," he said. Noncommittally.

"Well, this is me telling you the truth." And then . . . I had to ask, I had to be sure. "Is it okay with you? That I'm gay?"

He nodded solemnly. "Uh-huh."

"I need you to understand something here. Some people say it's a bad thing to be gay."

"Well, they're assholes." He declared it in a tone that left no room for argument.

I had to smother the urge to laugh out loud. "I agree with the sentiment, kiddo. But we're going to have to work on the language."

"If you're not all right with them, then they're not all right with me."

And that settled that. I couldn't have asked for a clearer statement. I gathered him into my arms and gave him a big, grateful hug. "I love you, sweetheart."

"I love you too," he said, giving me a strangle-hug in return.

On the way home, I asked, "Um . . . Dennis? When do you think you would like to start calling me Daddy?"

"When you start calling me son."

"Okay, son."

"Okay, Daddy."

It was that easy.

I looked at him with new eyes, tears of astonishment and joy blurring my vision. *He was my son now.*

~~~~~~~~~~~~~~~~~~~~~~

Oɴᴄᴇ ᴜᴘᴏɴ ᴀ ᴛɪᴍᴇ, I'ᴅ ʜᴀᴅ ᴛʜɪs fantasy, I wouldn't tell my mother anything at all about the impending adoption—then one day, I'd show up at her house with a little boy. She would look at him and ask, "Who's this?"

And I would reply, "Your new grandson." Just for the look on her face and the resulting shriek of surprise.

Of course, it couldn't work that way. The caseworkers needed to know that the extended family would be supportive of the adoption, so everybody had to be on board, even before they met the child.

On the other hand, telling a Jewish mother she has a new grandson, but can't meet him yet is almost as exquisite. On the scale of unbearable anticipation, it outranks the first trip to Disneyland. It's right up there with chocolate, redheads, and honeymoons.

Mom and Harvey lived fifteen minutes away. Three miles east, three miles south on the 405 freeway, two miles east on the 101—

Summer evenings in California are surly, with the hot breath of the wind breathing down the back of your neck like a giant Labrador retriever. In an open convertible, the air roars past, all dry and leathery. It always makes me think of Raymond Chandler's literary housewives fingering the edges of kitchen knives and studying their husbands' necks.

As we slid through the glimmering night, Dennis asked, "What's she making for dinner?"

Without missing a beat, I deadpanned, "Pickled mongoose."

I might just as well have switched on an air-raid siren: "I don't want pickled mongoose. I don't like pickled mongoose. I'm not eating pickled mongoose—"

"Have you ever had pickled mongoose? How do you know you don't like it if you've never had it?"

"I don't want pickled mongoose. I don't like pickled mongoose. I'm not eating pickled mongoose—"

"You'll take one taste. You'll try it. Maybe you'll like it. Grandma Jo makes the best pickled mongoose in the whole world. She does this thing with cobra sauce—"

"I don't want pickled mongoose. I don't like pickled mongoose. I'm not eating pickled mongoose—"

Uh-oh. He was taking me serious.

This was a double whammy. I wasn't used to people taking me serious. And worse, it meant that Dennis didn't understand jokes. Not good.

The ability to joke is the difference between sane people and crazy people. Crazy people don't do jokes. I wondered just how big a problem this was going to be.

"I DON'T WANT PICKLED MONGOOSE!"

By now, we were in serious risk of Dennis shattering large chunks of air out of the sky. I had no idea what the limits of his lung power might be. This could go on for days.

I remembered an old piece of engineering wisdom: "If you don't know where the OFF switch is, don't press the ON button." It applied to children too.

We got off the freeway at Van Nuys Boulevard. Turn right, turn left, turn left and we're there. Dennis was still going strong. Sooner or later, he would have to take a breath.

I let him out of the car and pointed him toward the rear

of the complex. "See those stairs? Grandma Jo and Grandpa Harvey live at the top." He rushed up the stairs ahead of me, then stopped and waited.

I knocked on the screen door and hollered, "Hello! Burglar—where do you hide the gold and jewelry?"

"Come on in. The gold is in the safe, the jewelry is under the bed."

Dennis followed me in. Grandma Jo was in the kitchen; she turned to us, wiping her hands on a towel. Dennis went straight to her, skipping all introductions. "What are you making for dinner?" he demanded.

"Chicken. And salad. And smashed potatoes."

"You're not making *pickled mongoose?*"

She didn't even blink. To her credit, she had always been fast on the uptake; it had only taken thirty years for her to figure out that her firstborn son was meshuga. (This may have been why there was no second-born son.) "Pickled mongoose? Oh, no." Dennis shot me a look of angry accusation. And then she added, "The store was all out of mongoose. I'll make it next time."

Dennis's expression turned back into a suspicious frown. He looked back and forth between us with narrowed eyes. Maybe he was starting to figure it out. I hoped so.

Harvey handed me a tumbler of scotch. I took a sip. The Chivas 100 blend. Not available in the States. I'd picked up two bottles at the duty-free store on my way back from England a year ago and given one to Harve for Father's Day. "Mmm, the good stuff. What's the special occasion?"

"You are."

"Well, we do have some news. Dennis, do you want to tell them?"

"David's gonna 'dopt me. He's gonna be my dad—and you're gonna be my Grandma and Grandpa!" He practically shouted the news.

"Oh, good," Mom said. "That means I get to hug you." She swept him into her arms and he grabbed her around the waist and held on tight. It was a perfect fit. Grandpa too. I couldn't tell who was happier. I promised myself this kid was going to spend a lot of time with his grandparents; it was all part of my secret plan to give him as many happy memories as possible.

And for a moment, I thought of my own Grandma. I hadn't realized until this moment how much a part of my life she'd been and how much I missed her . . . and how much she would have loved Dennis.

And then, of course, the inevitable Grandma moment. "Well, you must be very hungry. Sit down and I'll serve."

Dennis eyed his dinner suspiciously.

"Relax, it's chicken," I said. "Nobody can torture a chicken like your Grandma Jo. That was chicken, wasn't it, Mom?"

"That's what it said on the wrapper."

"I dunno . . . it tastes like rattlesnake to me. Doesn't it taste like rattlesnake to you, Dennis?"

"No!" he insisted. "It tastes like chicken!"

"Or maybe iguana?"

"Chicken!"

"I can make iguana for you sometime, then we'll see—"

"No!"

I decided not to pursue it. Probably a wise decision.

As soon as he finished eating, Dennis asked quietly, "Can I wash the dishes?"

My mother looked at me, eyebrows raised. *This is the monster child you were so worried about?* To Dennis, she said, "Of course, you can, sweetheart."

We watched as he very carefully cleared the table, taking all the dishes to the sink. He made three deliberate trips. Then he turned on the water and began sudsing and scrubbing.

"Do you rent him out?"

Very softly, I said, "He's trying to show us how much he wants to fit in. He's terrified it won't work."

"Of course, it's going to work," she said, not bothering to whisper. "He's a good kid."

Harvey added, "All you have to do is love him."

"Well, that's the game plan—"

"You're going to have to find a school for him," said Harvey.

"And he's going to need new clothes," said Mom. "Shoes, shirts, pants. What size is he? I'll take him to the mall—"

"Just a minute here," I interrupted. "If you want to spoil a kid, spoil your own. This one is mine."

Dennis walked out of the kitchen, a dish and a towel in his hand. His expression was serious. Very soft and very polite, he said, "She could spoil me if she wants to." His timing and delivery were perfect. He returned to the kitchen without further comment.

Mom and Harvey looked at him, then to me. Mom said, "I think you've met your match."

Harvey added, "He's going to fit into this family just fine."

"I think so."

"Does he ever smile?" Harvey asked softly.

"Give him time. He hasn't had a lot to smile about yet. That's first on my list of things to do."

~~~~~~~~~~~~~~~~~

On the day dennis moved in— *officially* moved in—Kathy told me she'd never seen him so happy. I asked her to remind him of that conversation he'd had with the counselor. "Remember when he said, 'I don't think God listens to my prayers.' Tell him that sometimes it takes God a little while to make a miracle happen."

Dennis brought with him a small, battered suitcase, half full of worn-out hand-me-downs; and a large cardboard box, less than half full of pieces of broken toys. His entire life could be carried in one trip.

Unpacking his few belongings was painful. Everything was tattered. Everything was precious. A too-small T-shirt autographed by Luc Robitaille and Wayne Gretsky. A sad and faded, dirty-with-age, stuffed gingerbread man named Eric.

A few photographs of a long-ago trip to the Los Angeles County Fair. The only evidence of a past. Not much evidence of a life, though.

He had only a few pairs of underpants. Three of them had pockets sewn onto the front. "What's this?" I asked.

"That's for the buzzer. If I wet the bed, it buzzes and wakes me up."

"We're not going to do that here," I said, tossing the underwear aside. "You won't be wearing those again." We put the T-shirts in one drawer, the shorts in another, and we were through unpacking.

"We can throw this out," I said, holding up his small, battered suitcase. It was pretty much falling apart.

"No," he said firmly. "I'll need it when I move out."

"No, you won't. You're not moving out. This is *it*."

"When I have to go back to Mars," he said. He took the suitcase from me and put it in the closet.

~~~~~~~~~~~~~~~~~~~~~~~~~~~~~

DENNIS NEEDED *EVERYTHING*.

We spent the week shopping.

Shoes. Underpants. T-shirts. Shorts. Socks. A jacket. A new teddy bear. Some storybooks for bedtime. Not too much, but enough. Christmas was coming soon; Santa was going to be very very good to this little boy.

It wasn't just his miracle, it was mine as well. I was terrified that it wasn't real, that somebody somewhere was going to realize that they'd made a horrible mistake placing him with me, and that suddenly one day, they'd come and pack him up and take him away, and the adventure would be over.

I spent the first three or four weeks with him in a state of absolute wonder that I had this marvelous little person in my life. I read him a story every night, tucked him into bed, hugged him, kissed him, told him how special he was to me, turned off the light and tiptoed out. I'd wait fifteen minutes, get a box of Kleenex, then tiptoe back in and sit and watch him sleep for an hour or two. It was better than television—and it was one of my few chances to see what he actually looked like. The rest of the time, he was mostly a blur with a smile.

I developed a routine for the mornings. First I'd turn to the little voice in my head that was muttering in amazement, "There's a seven o'clock in the morning too?" and say, "Thank you for sharing that, now shut up."

Then I'd wake Dennis up and before his blood sugar could remind him that he was hyperactive, I'd hand him a glass of orange juice and pop him into the tub and start a hot breakfast. Hot cereal. Or pancakes. Dennis loved pancakes. Or scrambled eggs and bacon. Toast and jelly. But no waffles. For Christmas, I'd bought a waffle iron that made waffles shaped like Mickey Mouse—but Dennis wouldn't eat any-thing that looked like a giant, grinning mongoose.

I gained five pounds. The last time I'd actually eaten breakfast, it had been an unwitting mistake—brought on by crossing the international date line on a sixteen-hour red-eye.

And then, one morning, right on schedule, it was time to test the rules. He decided he didn't want to eat breakfast. I told him he had to. He said no, and then abruptly he announced, "The adoption is off. I'm moving out." He went to the front door, walked out, and closed it behind him. I waited thirty seconds, then followed. He was standing on the front porch, waiting for me.

Very calmly, I said, "You can't move out until you finish breakfast."

So he came back in and ate.

As he was finishing, I said, "Why don't you go to school now, and you can move out after you get home from school, all right?"

He went to school.

When he got home from school, I handed him a peanut butter sandwich, and said, "Listen, why don't you wait and run away from home on the weekend. You can go farther."

I kept that up for three days, until he finally said, "I'm not going to run away from home." I made a note in my journal: *Sighted manipulation, sank same.*

I had a plan. Affirmations—lots of little reminders, like pebbles tossed into a pond, to let him know how much he was loved—that he was finally *connected*. And choices—opportunities to feel in control, to give him back a sense of power over his own life. The system had stolen that from him, yanking him around from place to place like a case file shuffled from desk to desk. And most of all, *a safe place* just to be—so he could have an emotional ground of being, and a sense that he wasn't alone anymore.

That last one would be the hardest to achieve.

The supermarket was always a challenge. He had to push the cart. No one else was allowed to touch it—Grand Prix de Vons. Up one aisle and down the next at Mach eight and a half. And always, strange things kept finding their way into the cart.

It amused me, how my shopping list had suddenly transformed. White bread instead of sourdough. Peanut butter. Jelly. Spaghetti. Tomato sauce. Hamburger. Cookies. Cheerios. Oatmeal. Cream of Wheat—that was my favorite when I was little. Malt-O-Meal. Ice cream. Hot dogs. Buns. Mustard, ketchup, relish. Chocolate for Daddy. Apples, bananas, grapes. Dog biscuits. "You and Somewhere will have to share these."

"I don't like dog biscuits."

"Then Somewhere will eat your share."

And in the middle of all this shopping, I had a flash of recognition—I was *being* Daddy. This was what it looked like. This was what it *felt* like.

Kewl.

I could get used to this. This was good.

On the drive home, I asked, "What should I make for dinner tonight? How about pickled mongoose?"

I should have known better—

"You're making fun of me!"

"Huh? No, I'm not!"

"I don't like it when people make fun of me! The kids at school used to make fun of me all the time. 'You live in a group home. You live in a group home.'"

I pulled the car over to the side. "I'm not making fun of you, sweetheart."

He was adamant. "Yes, you are!"

Sigh.

This part wasn't in the manual.

For some odd reason, I had a picture in my head of John F. Kennedy discovering that there were nuclear missiles in Cuba, in October of 1962. His reaction? "This is the day we earn our salary."

"Dennis, let me explain something to you about jokes. People don't tell jokes to make fun of each other. People tell jokes because they like each other. Jokes are a way of playing together."

"I don't like it! It feels like you're making fun of me! Everybody always makes fun of me!"

"Sweetheart, I'm not making fun of you. I will *never* make fun of you. You're my favorite kid in the whole wide world. And you need to learn something very important here. You're in a family of people who love to tell jokes. It's our way of saying, 'I love you, play with me.' So you're going to have to learn how to tell jokes too."

"I don't know any jokes—"

That stopped me for a moment. A kid who didn't know any jokes? "Okay, I'll teach you one."

He fell silent. I went rummaging frantically through the attics of memory for the easiest and silliest joke I knew.

"Okay, ready? Why do elephants have such big trunks?"

"I dunno."

"Because they don't have glove compartments."

"What's a glove department?"

Right.

We had a lot of work to do.

"See this thing here in front of you? It opens up. That's a glove compartment. It's called a glove compartment because you put gloves in it."

"I don't have any gloves."

"Nobody in California does. It's against the law. But the cars are all made in Detroit or Tokyo, where everybody wears gloves. So that's why they put glove compartments into cars. So now you know why elephants have such big trunks—"

"Because they don't have glove departments."

"Close enough. Very good. Now you tell that joke to everybody you meet."

"Will they laugh?"

"I'm sure they will. If they don't, we'll return the joke to the manufacturer and get a full refund."

For the next few weeks, he told that joke to everyone he saw—Grandma and Grandpa. Our neighbor, Roz. The waitress at the corner coffee shop. Julieanne, his therapist. Aunt Alice. Susie, my assistant. And it didn't even matter if he got it right. "Why don't elephants have glove departments? Because they have trunks." "Why don't elephants have trunks? Because they have glove departments." "Where do elephants put their gloves? In their trunks." And everybody he told it to laughed. Every time.

It was basic communication theory: jokes are a way of producing a happy response in people. If you want to be liked, tell jokes; it shows you want to play. And that's all that any of us really want—the chance to play together.

Dennis had been given one of the keys to the universe, and he was unlocking everything he could.

"Knock-knock."

"Who's there?"

"Orange?"

His eyes narrowed. "Orange who?"

"Orange you glad I didn't say *banana*?"

He made me sorry I taught him that one—I had to hear it a dozen times a day for the next two months. Some jokes are funny once. Some jokes are funny every time. It depends on who's telling them. But if you're only eight years old, it doesn't matter. The fun is in the telling, not the punch line. The fun is in the laughing.

And then one morning, while I was getting him ready for school—we were still only a few weeks into this adventure—*it* happened. I'd put him into the bathtub, a naked little toothpick of a child with puppy-dog eyes and Liz Taylor eye-lashes. A little bubble bath and he was happy. He could wash himself, but he liked being taken care of. I wondered if any-body had ever really taken care of him before.

Okay, time to go start some water boiling for hot cereal. I stopped and asked, "What do you want for breakfast? Cream of Wheat? Or Malt-O-Meal?"

He looked up at me, with an expression so innocent you could have used it as icing on a birthday cake. Very softly, very shyly, he said, "Pickled mongoose . . ." And waited for my reaction.

I blinked.

"Um—" For half an instant, I was annoyed, because he hadn't answered the question I'd asked, and then the enor-mity of what had just happened sank in. I grinned. "Okay. Pickled mongoose it is." And then, as an afterthought: "Do you want the Cream of Wheat flavored pickled mongoose or Malt-O-Meal flavor?"

"Cream of Wheat flavor."

"Okay, Cream of Wheat flavor pickled mongoose, coming right up." And we both smiled.

Halfway to the kitchen, in the middle of the hall, where not even the dog could see me, I stopped for a quick, silent victory dance, punching the air with both fists in a one-two triumph.

"*Yes!*"

That's what miracles look like.

V<small>ERY</small> QUICKLY, WE SETTLED INTO what passed for a routine.

Whenever Dennis came home from school, I always stopped what I was doing to give him the happiest greeting in the world. That was conscious and deliberate—this house would never be a place where he'd open the front door and get hit with a bitchy little "yick."

Somewhere and I would always hurry to greet him, one of us barking and the other one shouting, "Hey, you! Where's my hug? I missed you! It's too quiet around here."

And always, always, I kept dropping little pebbles of affirmation into the conversation: "Have I told you today how much I love you?" "You're my favorite kid in the whole wide world." "I'm so glad you picked me out." "What do you think about that?"

"It's good." Most of the time, he said it flat, without affect. Like he didn't really get it yet. Like that sullen *h'lo* on the first day.

Not a problem. Rome didn't fall in a day either.

Autumn left and took all the leaves with her. Winter arrived like ice cream, sweet and cold. Disney movies with a little boy sitting on my lap. Bedtime stories at night. An enormous pile of presents under the Christmas tree. Astonishment. "Is all that for me?"

"No. The red one is mine. The rest are yours."

By February, we had found our rhythm: special education school; extra attention from the teacher's aides. Snacks in the afternoon. Play therapist on Tuesday. Dinner with Grandma and Grandpa once a week. Movie on Saturday. Psychiatrist once a month; update the prescriptions. Wash the dishes, do the laundry, change the sheets, collapse exhausted into bed, get up the next morning—repeat until dead.

But there was also the dark side of the farce: Troubling fights with the kid next door. Parking-meter money disappearing from the ashtray in the car. Suspensions from school. Kitchen knives hidden under his mattress. Playing with matches. Lies and broken promises.

I told myself, the poor kid doesn't realize that he's in a different place yet. He's been moved around so many times to so many different places, how can he know? For so many years he's had no loyalty to anything but his own survival, how can I expect anything more from him? Whatever—the job at hand was to be the good dad that he wanted and needed, so I tried not to lose my temper. I walked him through the explanations patiently and hoped that he was hearing.

Sometimes, he acted out in the restaurant, in the supermarket, at the mall. Always in crowds. Why? Strangers looked at me as if the fault were mine—sometimes offering the advice of the ignorant and uninformed. Missing the backstory, they made their own assumptions. Did they deserve an explanation? No. And I refused to violate my son's privacy to give them any. So I held my tongue and didn't speak his past. And left them smoldering in their unspoken condemnations. In those moments, I felt trapped. The wild child runs amuck and makes the parent look crazy.

It made me doubt myself. A lot.

It was everything that had been promised in the books. In the tapes. In the seminars. In all the courses. If nothing else, I felt proud of myself for recognizing the pattern. At least, I knew what I was up against. At least, I wasn't caught by surprise. I hadn't been trapped by expectations of normalcy.

Once, in the mall, after I'd told him to stay with me—his ears must have been turned off again—he wandered away anyway. Not too far, but far enough to be worrisome. I caught up with him in a gift store and gave him a swat on the butt; not hard enough to hurt, just loud enough to get his attention. "What part of *stay with me* didn't you understand?" I marched him out of the store.

A moment later, an infuriated, red-faced woman confronted me, bawling me out. She blocked my way. "That's no way to treat a child!"

Big mistake. This was a family day. First, Cousin Jon stepped up to the woman, telling her politely to butt out. Bigger mistake—she got louder. A much bigger mistake because now Aunt Alice came diving in out of the sun, and Grandma came in on the flank. Hell hath no fury like an enraged grandmother. She rolled in like a rabid bulldozer.

I didn't see the rest of it. This was not a confrontation I

needed to have. And it was much more important that I turn Dennis around and march him away and around the corner.

All the ugly doubts came back, and this time they brought their cousins, the frightful worries. Was I screwing this up?

I looked at my son. He was fine. Just a bit puzzled. "What was that lady angry about?"

"She didn't think I should have swatted you on the butt."

"But that's your job. You're my dad. You're supposed to spank me when I'm bad."

"Do you know why I swatted you?"

"For not staying with you." And then he added. "It didn't hurt."

"It wasn't supposed to hurt. It was only supposed to get your attention." And then, embarrassed, I added, "And to let you know how angry I was that you hadn't listened."

"I know," he said, the angel child again.

"Thank you, sweetheart, for understanding." I hugged him, and that was the end of it. As puzzled as he was, he must have been privately pleased by all the fuss on his behalf. Hell, who wouldn't have been?

Later, I heard the rest of the story. The force of nature that we call Grandma Jo had erupted into classic street the-ater—"That man you're yelling at is my son. You have no idea how long and how hard he worked to adopt that boy. And you have no idea what that boy has been through. His mother abandoned him, the system failed him, and this is the first loving home he's ever been in. I am so proud of my son for the challenge he's taken on. And part of that is teaching the child some discipline now, before it's too late—otherwise he'll never learn it. You have no right to interfere where you don't know what's going on—" That was only the overture.

The crowd awarded her both ears and the tail.

I have no idea what happened to the poor woman. I assume she fled in embarrassment—or maybe she huffed off in a snit, carrying her anger away like a smoldering prize, to nurture it for months or even years afterward.

But after that, whenever we went out, we always hung a warning sign on Mom: **Beware: Grandma On Duty.**

More important, I never swatted him on the butt again.

~~~~~~~~~~~~~~~~~~~~~~~~~~~~

W<small>HEN</small> E<small>ASTER CAME AROUND, ONE</small> of the other children brought his new stuffed bunny to school to show off.

So Dennis had to have a stuffed bunny of his own. It was all he talked about.

I had a pretty good idea what was going on. He wanted to show that he had a dad too, who would buy him things. This child had wired it up that belongings were the measure of a person's goodness—especially clothes. *Especially* shoes.

He'd been teased by the children at his former school for always wearing hand-me-down clothes. The lesson had been well stamped in.

I resisted the bunny conversation for as long as I could. Two days. Three. But he was so insistent, *too* insistent.

Should I resist? Should I give in? If I was going to make a mistake, which way should I err? The answers to some questions do not crystallize easily. Was this the first step toward creating a truly spoiled child? Or was I fulfilling some necessary need? If this was about an emotional need, the answer was obvious. I sighed in resignation and took him to the toy store in the mall.

He picked out the biggest blue bunny he could hold. It had a great expression—big, friendly eyes and a big, goofy smile—and we both agreed it was the best bunny in the store. And yes, it was bigger than the other kid's bunny.

He took it to school the next day to show off. Classic one-upmanship. I didn't like the game, but after eight years, this little guy was entitled to win one round at least.

Later, I asked the therapist about it. Was I spoiling him? She said that if I was going to err, it was better to be too generous than not enough. That was good enough for me. I stopped worrying about it.

He put the bunny in the place of honor at the head of his bed and slept with it every night. Between the bunny and the dog, there wasn't a lot of room left for kid, but the three of them were very happy together.

~~ ~~ ~~ ~~ ~~ ~~ ~~ ~~ ~~ ~~ ~~ ~~

Mosт of тне тıмe, wнen stran-gers ask me what I do, I tell them I teach.

Two reasons. If I tell them I write, they always ask what I write. And if I tell them *what* I have written, either they're going to say, "Never heard of it," or they're going to say, "You wrote *that?*" and I'm trapped in a rerun of a dialog I stopped having two decades ago. Either way, it's not a conversation I want to have.

"I teach remedial English," which wasn't exactly a lie. The uneven quality of students enrolled in my evening screenwriting class at Pepperdine more than justified jokes about the Malibu Institute for the Melanin Deficient.

The other reason for not admitting to earning a living by writing is that it's like telling people you're either a psychiatrist or a priest. You get to watch them pretend to be sane and sinless for the rest of the evening—which is great fun at cocktail parties, but an absolute bore in a singles bar.

And then of course, there's always the inevitable proposition: "Hey, I've got this really great idea for a book. If you'll type it up, I'll split the money with you."

I'd finally figured out the perfect answer to that ploy: "That's a great idea. Okay, you do the first draft and I'll polish it."

Nobody has ever followed through, but I still live in fear that someday, 537 dreadful first drafts are all going to show up in my mailbox, all on the same day. . . .

I guess, in the excitement, I'd forgotten to explain to Dennis what I did for a living. He knew I worked at home, muttering at a computer screen full of big words, but that seemed to be the limits of his understanding. Every other adult he'd ever lived with had been a full-time caregiver; taking care of kids had been their only job. The idea that a parent actually had to *work* for a living hadn't occurred to him yet.

One day, I was folding towels and T-shirts in my bedroom. Dennis came in, carrying the last armload of laundry from the dryer; he dumped it on the bed. Usually, he helped with the folding, but today his attention was drawn to the bookshelf. He began taking books out at random and looking at them curiously.

Ordinarily, I would have reminded him that he had to help with the chores—but if he was getting interested in books, I wasn't going to discourage him. And besides, these were books I had written.

"Did you *read* all these books?" he asked. The inevitable question of the nonreader.

"Even worse. I *wrote* all those books."

He gave me a look of disbelief. *"Nuh-uh!* No, you didn't!"

I reached past him and plucked a hardcover off the shelf. I dropped it into his hands. "See, my name is on the cover."

"What's it about?" he demanded.

"It's about a man with a time machine built into his belt, so he can go back in time and talk himself out of making mistakes."

"That's a good idea," he said.

"Maybe. But if you always talk yourself out of making mistakes, then you won't do anything at all. And you won't learn anything either. Mistakes are a great teacher. That's why I'm so smart. I make lots of mistakes."

Dennis turned the book over and looked at the picture on the back cover. Oops. Bad idea, picking that book. The photograph had been taken in 1972. . . . Shoulder-length hair. Loud shirt. Bell-bottoms. Thank God it was in black-and-white.

"Who's this?"

"That's one of my mistakes. That's me. A long time ago."

"No, it isn't!"

"Okay, it isn't. It was a guy who used to dance at Chippendale's. We hired him to pose for the picture."

"No, you didn't! Do you still have the shirt? Can I wear it?"

"The fashion police would arrest me. And the Department of Children's Services would say I'm abusing you."

"I mean for Halloween."

"I don't think you want to be that scary." I took the book from him and put it back on the shelf. "Come on, it's time to get ready for bed."

As I helped him into his pajamas, he asked, "How do you write a book?"

"I sit and I type." It was an old writer's koan, told to me by an old writer: *Apply the seat of the pants to the seat of the chair.* And now that I was an old writer too, I understood it better than ever.

"No. I mean, how do you know what to type?"

"I'll show you." I sat down on his bed and pulled him into my lap—the bedtime story position.

"Do we need a computer?"

"No, that part comes later. First we have to imagine something."

"How?"

"You know how to imagine, don't you?" He shook his head. "Yes, you do. You just don't know it yet. Here. Close your eyes. Come on, close your eyes, and I'll ask you questions and you tell me what you see. Okay, ready? Once upon a time, there was a little boy. And his name was . . . ? His name was . . . ?"

"Dennis!"

"Right. And Dennis lived . . . where?"

"On Mars."

"Mars. Yes, that's good. I like Mars. And Mars looks like . . . ?"

"It's red. All red. And lots of rocks."

"All red. Lots of rocks. And?"

"And . . . it's very dry. All the water is frozen in the rocks. And it's very cold there, but it's so dry you can't freeze. You just stop and wait. Everybody on Mars waits. That's all they do." Eyes still closed, he frowned as if looking at something else inside his head. "They've been waiting so long, nobody knows how long. Everything on Mars is so old even the rocks don't remember how old. And they've been waiting all that time."

He startled me. Monosyllabic Dennis had suddenly turned poetic. It made me wonder—

"Go on," he prompted. "What's next?"

"Right. Okay. Let's see. Well, in this story, there was something Dennis wanted."

"What?"

"You have to tell me. What did Dennis want?"

"Strawberries. Dennis wanted to eat strawberries."

"And there are no strawberries on Mars, right?

"Uh-huh."

"Okay, so he had to do what . . . ?"

"Go get the strawberries."

"Right. So where did he have to go?"

"To David's house."

I laughed. "Works for me. See how easy that is? That's how you write a story."

Dennis opened his eyes. "That's not a real story."

"Sure, it is."

"No, it isn't."

"Okay, why not?"

"Nothing happened."

I sighed. "Everybody's a critic." I gave him a hug. "But you're right. A story needs a problem to solve. Close your eyes again and imagine a big problem." I gave him a moment. "Dennis wants to eat strawberries, but he can't eat strawberries because why?"

"The bad lady won't let him."

"And the bad lady's name is . . . ?"

"*PattheFuckingBitch*." He said it calmly.

Oops. What did I just step in?

Yes, I knew about Pat; Kathy Bright had told me how he'd had to testify against her when he was four years old. He'd been terrified. Pat had done a lot of bad things to him, more than he was ever able to communicate.

I'd made a rule for myself not to pry into his past. If he wanted to tell me, I'd listen. But I wasn't going to force him to talk about anything that made him uncomfortable. He didn't need me to be a therapist, but a dad. The only history I wanted to know was the history we were making together. He needed happy memories to live in. So did I.

"Uh—okay. Um . . . That's really not a good word to use in a story. How about we call her 'Pat, the wicked witch?'"

Dennis opened his eyes. "But she isn't a wicked witch. She's a *FuckingBitch*."

"I know, sweetheart. But sometimes in a story, you change things."

"Why?"

Good question. I'd often wondered that myself.

"Because it works better," I said, not really liking the answer.

"But it's *my* story."

"You're right. Okay, so we have Pat the um . . . whatever. Close your eyes again now." *Let's see where this is going.* "And . . . what does Dennis do to her?"

"I know! He *disneygrades* her."

"He *disneygrades* her?"

"He's a Martian. So he points his disneygrader at her—"

Dennis opened his eyes and showed me his "disneygrader." He pointed with his fist, index and little finger extended like horns, only vertical instead of horizontal. "And he goes *brtrtrtrt!!* And she *melts!*"

"Into a puddle of green slime, right?"

"No, red slime."

"And then what happened?"

"He ate her all up and it made him sick, so he threw up. And he was sick in bed for eighty-seven days."

"Well, there's a good lesson for you. Don't eat red slime. But I thought he wanted strawberries."

"Yeah, that too."

"So, where's the strawberries?"

"In the refrigerator. And I'm going to eat them."

"With lots of whipped cream, I'll bet. That's what we'll have for dessert tomorrow, okay?"

"Okay."

"There. See? That's how you write a story. First you make it up. Then you write it down." I rocked him gently in my arms. "The making up is the fun part. Did you like imagining your story?"

"Yeah," he admitted.

"I've got an idea," I said. "If you want to imagine a story of your own, you can. You can type it up on my other computer, and I'll print it out for you, just like one of mine."

"In a book?"

"First write the story, then we'll worry about finding a publisher. . . ."

A FEW DAYS LATER, HE DID WRITE A story. It was called "Dark."

It was a dark night once a little boy got mad and ran away from his famlie.

He got lost in a dark forist.

There were monsters hiding in the dark forist gust waiting for the boy to come closer and closer in tell the boy was clos a nufe that they could get him.

And one day they did.

So the boy learnd never to run from home again becas he knew the monsters would go searching for him again so he walked bake home to his famile and they missed him so much and so the boy never ran away again from his famile but then he went back into the forist and the monsters were looking for Him and before He could turn around a monster cameout and grabed him and took him to there dongen were they were going to cook Him but in a big humunges and the most bigest pot he had ever seen in hole life BUT HE MANedg To GEt OUt ANd Run AWAy ANd RUn HOMe and his famile missed him so much they all gave him a big hug but the monsters manedg to get in and the famlie ran as fast as they coud and got away and the monsters tared up there home but the monsters were gone looking for them and the famlie had emergency hide out and infact they got to use it and it had a refrigarater in it and surevived in it and they always would go out and look to see if the monsters were still runing a round and one day the monsters new that the famlie would not come out ever again ever ever ever ever ever ever ever ever ever ever ever again so the monsters went back in the forrost just waiting it's next hostage and but the famile came out one day just one day after they new the monsters were gone and the family came back out to eat some good food they had in there refriderator at home.

Then the boy grew up to be a orc he liked being a orc but his parents didn't like the fact of there son being a orc but he was what he was hay whoe says everone is perfect huh? I met this weird kid and I liked him we went to sschool together and went over to each others house all the time. I liked the fact that he was an orc because it was kida funnie infact the first time I met him It was weird really weird totall weird so weird I could not resist it it was so cool I liked meeting him he's my best friend well one of them. One day I waas walking home and I said to him I liked the old times but now it's also is cool now to you know!!!!

A MIRACLE, ACCORDING TO MY friend Randy MacNamara, is *something that wouldn't have happened anyway*.

After the fact, after the first giddy days of panic and joy, after the days of bottomless fears, after the tantrums and the testing, after a thousand and one peanut butter and jellyfish sandwiches, I understood what he meant.

A miracle takes commitment. It never happens by accident.

I'd had other miracles happen in my life—one which I'd written about, one which I may never write about—but this one was the best. I had the proof of it framed on my wall.

One afternoon I'd opened Dennis's lunch kit to see how much he'd eaten, I found the note I'd packed that morning. It said, *Please eat your whole lunch today! I love you! Daddy.*

On the other side, written in a childish scrawl, was Dennis's reply:

I love you to. you are very specil to me. I realy think your the best. I love you very much dady I never

loved eneyone more than you. I never new anyone
nicer than you.

At the bottom, he'd drawn three hearts and put the word
dady in the biggest of them.

So the miracle was complete. Dennis *could* form a deep
attachment. And he could express it. And all I had to do was
sit and glow and realize that despite all my doubts and all my
mistakes, I was getting the important part of the job done
right. I had passed from wannabe to gonnabe to finding-how-
to-be to simply *being*.

And that was a pretty good way to be.

~~~~~~~~~~~~~~~~~~~~~~~~~~~~~~

I HAD FORGOTTEN ALL ABOUT MAR-
tians.

Seven months later we were in Arizona, at a party at Jeff
Duntemann's sprawling house.

Jeff is a two-time Hugo nominee who gave up science fiction to write books about computer programming. Apparently, it was far more profitable than science fiction; now he
was publishing his own magazine, *PC-Techniques*. I had been
writing a column for the magazine since issue number one,
an off-the-wall mix of code and mutated Zen.

I was sitting on the patio, watching Dennis hurling himself in sparkling cannonballs into the deep end of the pool. A year before, I couldn't pry him loose from the steps in the shallow end; now he was an apprentice fish. He spent more time swimming across the bottom of the water than the top. And me—I was glowing as brightly as the warm Arizona evening. Pink clouds were striped across the twilight sky. It was country to fall in love with.

I didn't know anyone else at the party besides Jeff and Carol—and the world-famous Mr. Byte, who was in the kitchen begging scraps he wasn't supposed to have—but that was all right; I was content just to sit and watch my son enjoy himself. The first stars were starting to come out and I was thinking about space, because I always thought about space when I looked out at the stars. In my imagination, I was already leaping out to other worlds—

—and then I heard the word *Martian* in back of me, and without moving at all, my attention swiveled 180 degrees.

Four of the wives were sitting together—it was that kind of party; the programmers were talking code, the wives were talking children. I didn't know enough about either subject. I still felt like a dabbler in both fields, so I made the best kind of listener.

One of the women was saying, "No, it's true. Since she was old enough to talk she's insisted she's a Martian. Her mother has never been able to convince her otherwise. She asked her, 'How do you explain that I remember going to the hospital and giving birth to you?' and she said, 'I was implanted in your tummy.' She's twelve now and she still believes it. She has a whole story, an explanation for everything. She says UFOs are implanting Martian babies all the time."

The other women laughed gently. I found myself smiling to myself and watching Dennis. Remembering for the first time in a long while what he'd once told his caseworker—that he was a Martian too. Interesting coincidence.

Then, one of the others said, "We had a boy in my daughter's class who wore a T-shirt to school almost every day that said, *I am a Martian*. He took a lot of teasing about it. The principal tried to make him stop wearing it, but he refused. All the kids thought he was crazy."

"That was probably the only way he could get the attention he needed."

"Well," said the fourth voice, "it's a common childhood fantasy—that the child is really a changeling or an orphan and that you're not her real mother. Adding Mars to it is just a way to take advantage of the real world to make it more believable."

I didn't hear any more of that conversation; we were interrupted by Carol announcing that dinner was served. I called Dennis out of the pool and wrapped him in a towel. He looked human to me—but maybe that was just the Martian mind-control trick.

"Did you have fun?" I asked.

"Yes," he said, noncommittally. He said everything non-committally.

"Then show me your having-fun face."

He turned to face me and gave me his biggest smile, a little bit forced, but definitely a smile.

"Okay, put on your hungry face and go frighten a hamburger."

The happy-face game had long since taken on a life of its own. Once, in a restaurant, we'd been waiting too long for our food to arrive and Dennis had started complaining. I said, "Maybe they don't know how hungry you are. Put on your hungry face. Your hungriest face ever."

Dennis's eyes lit up, and he licked his chops—just like Somewhere. If I'd been a dog biscuit, I'd have feared for my life.

"Oh, that's very good. Now show me your I'm-so-sad-I'm-going-to-cry face."

That one was his very best. It was the lost-orphan expression. Put it on a collection can and you can raise a thousand dollars an hour. He'd used it on me to great effect more than once.

"Show me the face you make when you find that your puppy has pooped in your shoe."

His expression turned yicky, then angry, then unhappy. I laughed, and so did he. And then our food arrived.

We played that game a lot—it was something to do when there wasn't anything else to do. The more inventive I became, the more Dennis revealed a startling talent for mimicry. One day, I said, "Show me your monkey face."

He thought for a moment, then puffed up his cheeks and pushed his ears forward so they stuck out from his head. He looked like a little pink chimpanzee. *"Eep, eep, eep,"* he said, and hopped around like a monkey.

"That was *good*. You'd better not do that next time we go to the zoo—they'll want to keep you."

Later, I realized how useful a game it really was for him. Dennis had never known how to be emotionally appropriate—growing up, surrounded by other abused and troubled children, his feelings were all skewed. This game was a kind of training. He hadn't known how he was supposed to *be*. And now that I'd given him a clue, I began to see him trying on new ways to be, trying on his emotions like choosing clothes to wear for school. He was slowly figuring it out—

—like he was learning how to be human.

~~~~~~~~~~~~~~~~~~~~~~~~~

THE NEXT DAY WE WERE SLICING across the desolate red desert, seemingly suspended between the blazing sky and the shimmering road, not talking about anything, sipping sodas from the cooler, and listening to a tape of Van Dyke Parks singing about how much he loved his son. The tape came to an end and the white noise of the wind rushed in to envelop us. Convertibles are fun, but they aren't quiet.

"Hey," I said.

"Hey," he answered.

"You know something?"

"What?"

"You're my favorite kid in the whole world."

"Yeah, I know."

"Oh, well, then I don't have to tell you, do I?"

"Yes, you do. That's your job."

"Oh, right. Thanks for reminding me."

We drove on a little farther. Abruptly, I remembered last night's conversation.

"Hey," I said.

"Hey," he answered.

"Are you a Martian?"

He hesitated.

"Are you a Martian?" I repeated.

"Why do you want to know?"

"Ah, obviously you're a Jewish Martian. You answer a question with a question."

"Who told you I was a Martian?"

"Kathy did. Before I met you, we had a meeting. She told me all about you. She said that you told her you were a Martian. Do you remember telling her that?"

"Yes."

"Are you still a Martian?"

"Yes," he admitted.

"Do you want to tell me about it?"

For a moment, he didn't say anything. Just as I was beginning to think that he wasn't going to answer at all, he spoke quietly. "I was made on Mars. I was a tadpole. Then I was brought to Earth in a UFO and implanted in my Mommy's tummy. She didn't know. Then I was borned."

"Ahh," I said. "That's how I thought it happened. Is that all?"

"Uh-huh."

"Why did the Martians send you here?"

"So I could be a Earth boy."

"Oh. That makes sense."

"Can we go to Round Table Pizza for dinner?" he asked, abruptly changing the subject as if it was the most natural thing to do.

"Do Martians like pizza?"

"Yes!" he said excitedly. Then he pointed his fingers at me like a funny kind of ray gun. Most children would have pointed the top two fingers to make a pretend gun, but Dennis pointed his index and little fingers, his thumb stood straight up for the trigger—the same way as when he'd told me his Martian story. "If you don't take me out for pizza tonight, I'll have to disneygrade you."

"Ouch, that sounds painful. I definitely do not want to be disneygraded. Then I'd have to stand in the dark and sing that awful song forever while boatloads of Japanese tourists take pictures of me. But we're not going tonight. Maybe tomorrow, if you have a good day at school."

"No, tonight!" He pointed his fingers menacingly—both hands now—and for a moment I wondered what would happen if he pressed his thumbs forward. Would I be turned into a giant three-fingered mouse?

"If you disneygrade me," I said, "for sure you won't get any pizza."

"Okay," he said. Then he closed up both weapons, first one hand, then the other. First the little finger of his left hand, then the index finger; then the little finger of his right hand, then the index finger. Each time he made a soft, clicking sound with his mouth. Finally he folded his thumbs down—and abruptly he had hands again.

Later, I tried to do the same thing myself. A human can do it, but it's like the Vulcan salute. It takes practice.

~~~~~~~~~~~~~~~~~~~~~~~~~

I HAVE A PINCHED NERVE IN MY BACK. If I do my twisting exercises a couple of times a week, and if I take frequent breaks from the keyboard, and if I remember to put myself into the spa every couple days and let the bubbles boil up around me, then I can keep myself functioning pretty much like a normal person. It's a fair trade. Usually I wait until after dinner to sit in the spa.

Several days after the Phoenix trip, Dennis and I were alone in the pool. The pool has a blue filter over the light; the spa has a red one, and when the bubbles are on, it looks like a hot lava bath. Sometimes we talk about nothing important. Sometimes we just sit silently, letting the air jets pummel us forever. And sometimes we stare up into the sky and watch for meteors; once we'd seen a bright red starpoint streak across the sky like a bullet.

But tonight, as he splashed in the bubbles, I found myself studying the way the light shaped his features. I'm not an expert on the development of children's skulls, but abruptly I was struck by the odd proportions of his forehead and eyes.

Before I'd adopted him, I'd been given copies of various doctors' reports. One doctor, who was supposed to be looking for fetal alcohol effects, had described the five-year-old Dennis as "an unusual-looking" child. I couldn't see what he was talking about.

To me, Dennis had always been an unusually good-looking boy. He was blessed with dark blond hair, which was growing steadily toward shoulder-length. His eyes were puppy-brown and hidden behind lashes long enough to trouble the sleep of mascara manufacturers. His complexion was as luminous and gold as an Arizona sunset.

His body was well-proportioned too; he had long legs and a swimmer's torso. He was thin, but not skinny, not anymore.

He looked like a Disney child. I expected him to be a heart-breaker when he grew up. The girls were going to chase him with lassos. Already I wondered what kind of a teenager he would become—and if I would be able to handle it.

Now . . . seeing him in the reflected red light of the spa—is this the same color light they have on Mars?—he did look a little *alien* to me. His forehead had a roundish bulge toward the crown. His cheekbones seemed strangely angled. His eyes seemed narrow and reptilian. Probably it was the effect of the light coming from underneath instead of above, and combined with the red filter, it was momentarily unnerving. For a moment, I wondered what kind of *thing* I'd brought into my life.

"What?" he asked, staring back.

"Nothing," I said.

"You were looking at me."

"I was admiring you. You're a beautiful kid, do you know that?"

"Uh-huh." And suddenly he was Dennis again.

"How do you know that?"

"Everybody says so. They all like my eyelashes."

But for that one moment, he hadn't been Dennis the little boy. He'd been something else. Something cold and watchful. And he'd noticed me studying him. He'd sensed the suspicion. Or was it just the power of suggestion at work? Most of the books on parenting advise you not to feel guilty for wondering if your child is suddenly going to catch a fly with his tongue. It's a very common parental fear.

I had doubts about Dennis. That was normal. When I confessed my fear that I would screw up, Randy MacNamara had said, "Well, let me put your mind at ease. You *are* going to screw up. The real question is whether or not you're going to forgive yourself and move on. Children are resilient. Are you?"

All I had to do was ask myself one easy question: How would I feel if Kathy Bright said she had to remove him from my home? *Ripped apart* was the simplest answer. The truth was, I didn't care if he was a Martian or not, I was as *bonded* to him as he was to me.

But . . . out of curiosity, and possibly just to reassure myself—that I was imagining things—I logged onto CompuServe. The ISSUES forum had a parenting section. I left a message under the heading, "Is your child a Martian?"

My little boy says he's a Martian. I've heard of two other children who claim to be Martians as well. Has anyone else heard of children who believe that they're from Mars?

Over the course of the next few days—before the message scrolled off the board and into the bit-bucket—I received thirty-three replies.

Several of the messages were thoughtful analyses of why a child might say such a thing. It was pretty much what that mother in Phoenix had surmised: it's common for children to fantasize that they have glamorous origins. In the past, children might have believed they were secretly princes and princesses, and one day their real parents would arrive to take them to their golden castles. But because that mythology has now been superseded by starships and mutants, it's more appropriate for children to fantasize about traveling away on the *Millennium Falcon* or the *Enterprise*. If a child was experienced enough to know that those stories were just fiction, he would also know that Mars was a real planet. Therefore . . . Mars gave credibility to the fantasy. Et cetera. Et cetera. Local mileage may vary, but if the delusion persists, see a good therapist. It may be evidence of some deeper problem. Et cetera some more.

I knew where Dennis's deeper problems came from. He'd been bounced around the foster care system for eight years before landing in my arms. He didn't know *where* he came from or *where* he belonged.

Several of the replies I received were from other parents sharing pieces of weirdness their own children had demonstrated. Interesting, but not particularly useful to my inquiry.

But . . . there were over a dozen private messages.

My sister's little girl used to insist that she'd been brought to Earth in a UFO and implanted in her mommy's tummy while her mommy was asleep. She kept this up until she was about fourteen, then abruptly stopped. After that, she wouldn't answer questions about it at all.

My next-door neighbors had a boy who said he wasn't from Earth. He disappeared when he was twelve. Without a trace. The police assumed he was kidnapped.

My ex-wife was a child psychologist. She used to joke about her Martian children. She said she could tell how crazy New York was by the number of Martians she saw in any given year. At first she used to tell the parents that same-old same-old about children needing to fantasize about a glamorous background, but later on she began to wonder. The stories the kids told were all very similar. They began life as Martian tadpoles brought to Earth and implanted in the uteruses of Earth women. She always wanted to do a study on Martian children, but she could never get a grant.

I dated a girl once who said she was from Mars. She was very insistent on it. When I tried to get serious with her, she turned me down flat. She said she really liked me, but it wouldn't work out between us. When I asked her why, she said it was because she was from Mars. That's all. I guess Martians have a rule against marrying outside their species.

I heard about a Martian when I was in high school. He killed himself. I didn't know him. I only heard about it afterward.

I thought I was from Mars once. I even had memories of being on Mars. It had a pink sky. That's how I knew it was Mars. When the photos came in from the Jet Propulsion Laboratory showing that Mars really did have a pink sky, just like in my memories, I thought that proved something. When I told my parents, they took me to see a doctor. I was in therapy for a long time, but I'm fine now. Maybe you should get your son into therapy.

It was the last one that got to me. I knew the person who sent it meant to be reassuring. Instead, the message had the opposite effect.

Okay, maybe it's me. Maybe it's because I'm a writer. I read subtext everywhere, even where none is intended. And maybe the cumulative effect of all these messages—especially the wistful, almost plaintive tone of the last one—left me with a very uncomfortable feeling.

I replied to the private messages.

I know this sounds silly, but please indulge me. What did your Martian friend/relative look like? Did he/she have any special physical characteristics or medical

problems? What was his/her personality like? Do
you know what happened to him/her? Does he/she
still believe that he/she is from Mars?

It took a week or two to compile the responses. Of the ten
Martians specifically mentioned, two had committed suicide.
One was successful in business. Three refused to talk about
Mars. Two were "cured." The whereabouts of the others
were unknown. Three were missing. Two of the missing had
been repeated runaways during their teen years. I wondered
where they thought they were running to.

Of the ten Martians, six were known to have had golden-
brown skin, round faces, brown eyes, and very long eyelashes.
The hair color was generally dark blond or brown. That was
an interesting statistical anomaly.

Of the ten Martians, five were hyperactive, two were
epileptic. The other three weren't known.

I asked the fellow whose ex-wife had been a child psychologist if she'd ever noticed any statistical patterns among her
Martians. He said he didn't know and he didn't even know her
whereabouts anymore. She had disappeared two years earlier.

I CALLED MY FRIEND, STEVE BARNES. He'd written one of the character references I'd needed to adopt Dennis, and because of that I regarded him as an unofficial godfather to the boy. We chatted about this and that and the other thing for a while. And then, finally, I said, "Steve—do you know about the Martian phenomenon?" He didn't. I told him about it. He asked me if I was smoking dope again.

"I'm serious, Steve."

"So am I."

"I haven't touched that crap since I kicked out she-who-must-not-be-named." I said it angrily.

"Just checking. You gotta admit that's a pretty bizarre story, though."

"I know that. That's why I'm telling you. You're one of the few people I know who will actually consider it fairly. Geez—why is it that science fiction writers are the most skeptical animals of all?"

"Because we get to deal with more crazies than anyone else," Steve replied, without missing a beat.

"I don't know what to do with this," I said, admitting my frustration. "I know it sounds like one more crazy UFO mystery. Only this one is something that can actually be validated. This is the kind of statistical anomaly that can't be explained away by coincidence. And I bet there's a lot more to it too. Like, what was the blood type of all those children? What was the position of the Earth and Mars when they were conceived? What was the phase of the moon? What are their favorite foods? How well did they do in school? What if there's something really going on here? Okay, maybe not Martians, maybe some kind of social phenomenon or syndrome—I don't know what it is, I don't know what else to ask, and I don't know who to tell. Most of all, I don't want to end up on the front page of the *Enquirer*. Can't you just see it? **SCI-FI WRITER HAS MARTIAN CHILD!**"

"It might be good for your career," Steve said thoughtfully. "I wonder how many new readers you would pick up."

"Oh, yeah, sure. And I wonder how many old readers I'd lose. I'd like to be taken seriously in my old age. Remember what happened to what's-his-name."

"Yeah, I'll never forget what's-his-name. That was a real sad story."

"Anyway. . . . Do you see my point? Where do I go from here?"

"You want my *real* advice?" Steve asked. He didn't wait for my reply. "Don't go anywhere with it. Drop it. Let someone else figure it out. Or no one. You said it yourself, David, more than once. 'It's almost always dangerous to be right too soon.' Don't go borrowing trouble. Turn it into a story if you must and let people think it's a harmless fantasy. But don't let it screw up your life. You wanted this kid, didn't you? Now you have him. Just parent him. That's the only thing that's *really* wanted and needed."

He was right. I knew it. But I couldn't accept it. "That's easy for you to say. You don't have a Martian in the house."

"Yes, I do." He laughed. "Only mine's a girl."

"Huh—?"

"Don't you get it? *All* children are Martians. We get thirteen years to civilize the little monsters. After that, it's too late. Then they start eating our hearts out."

"You sound like my mother now."

"I'll take that as a compliment."

"It's a good thing you don't know her, or you wouldn't say that. People don't turn out like me by accident."

"Listen to me, David," and his tone of voice was so serious that six different jokes died before they could pass my lips. "You're right on schedule. Have you ever really looked at the faces of new parents? Most of them are walking around in a state of shock, wondering what happened. It's part of the process of assimilation. The only difference is that you have a more active imagination than most people. You know how to name your fears. Trust me on this, Toni and I went through it with Nicki. We thought she was a—never mind. Just know this is normal. There are days when you are absolutely certain that you've got a cute and stinky little alien in your house."

"But *every* day?"

"Trust me. It passes. In a year or two, you won't even remember what your life was like before."

"Maybe that's how long it takes a Martian to brainwash its human hosts. . . ."

Steve sighed. "You've got it bad."

"Yes, I do," I admitted.

~~~~~~~~~~~~~~~~~~~~~~~~

The Martian thing gnawed at me like a mouse in my mental attic. I couldn't get it out of my head. No matter what we did, the thought was there.

If we went out front to swat koosh-balls back and forth, I wondered if the reason he was having trouble with his coordination was the unfamiliar gravity of Earth. If we went in the backyard and jumped in the pool together, I wondered if his attraction to water was because it was so scarce on Mars.

I wondered about his ability to hear a piece of music a single time and still remember the melody so clearly that he could sing it again, note for note, a month later. He would walk through the house singing songs that he could not have heard except on the tapes I occasionally played. How many nine-year-olds know how to sing "My Clone Sleeps Alone" like Pat Benatar?

I wondered why he had so little interest in comic books,

but loved to watch television dramas about the relationships of human beings. He hated *Star Trek;* he thought it was "too silly." He loved the Discovery channel—especially all the shows about animals and insects.

There was no apparent pattern to his behavior, nothing that could be pointed to as evidence of otherworldliness. Indeed, the fact that he was making his father paranoid was a very strong argument that he was a normal Earth kid.

Except . . . every time I started to forget . . . something would happen. Maybe he'd react to something on television with an off-the-wall comment that would make me look over at him curiously. Like that Bugs Bunny cartoon, for instance, where the rabbit is making life miserable for Marvin the Martian, stealing the eludium-235 detonator so he can't blow up the Earth. In the middle of it, Dennis quietly declared, "No, that's wrong. Martians aren't like that." Then he got up and turned the television set *off.*

"Why did you do that?" I asked.

"Because it was wrong," he said blandly.

"But it's only a cartoon." One of my *favorite* cartoons, I might add.

"It's still wrong." And then he turned and went outside as if the whole concept of television would never be interesting to him again.

And now, almost two years to the day since I'd filled out the first application, the nickel finally dropped and I sat up in bed in the middle of the night. Why were so many adopted children *hyperactive?*

The evidence was all around me. I just hadn't noticed it before. It was there in the photo-listing books. It seemed as if every third child was hyperactive. It was acknowledged in the books, the articles, the seminars, the tapes . . . that a higher proportion of foster children have attention deficit disorder, also called hyperactivity. Why was that?

Some theorists suggested that it was the result of substance abuse by the parents, which is why we saw it more in abandoned and unwanted children. The doctors said that hyperactivity was the result of the body's failure to produce certain key enzymes in response to physical stimulation, therefore, the child needed to overstimulate himself in order to produce an equivalent amount of calming; but others postulated that there was an emotional component to the disorder—that it was a response to a lack of nurturing.

Most interesting of all to me was the offhand note in one article that some theorists believed that many cases of ADHD were actually misdiagnoses. If you were unattached and didn't know who you were or where you had come from or where you were going, you'd have a lot to worry about; your attention might be distracted too.

Or . . . what if the behavior that was judged abnormal for Earth children was perfectly normal for Martian children? What if there was no such thing as ADHD in Martians?

At this point, I'd reached the limits of my ability to research the question. Who could I tell? Who would have the resources to pursue this further? And who would take me seriously?

There was simply no way for me to research this question without destroying all of my credibility as a writer.

Even worse, *there was no way to research it without also destroying my credibility as a parent.*

Kathy Bright came by once a month to check on our progress. Up until this time, I'd always been candid with her. The same with the therapist and the psychiatrist. I'd talked to them about all the little discipline problems, the inappropriate behaviors and my feelings of frustration, and especially about every little step in the right direction and every little victory.

But this was something I *couldn't* talk to them about. Suppose I called Kathy Bright. What could I say? "Uh, Kathy, it's David. I want to talk to you about Dennis. You know how he says he's a Martian? Well, I think he might *really* be a Martian and . . ."

Uh-huh.

If the adoptive father was starting to have hallucinations

about the child, how long would the Department of Children's Services leave the child in that placement? About twenty minutes, I figured. About as long as it took to get out there and pick him up. She'd pull him out of my house so fast they'd be hearing sonic booms in Malibu. And she'd be right to do so. A child needs a stable and nurturing environment. How stable and nurturing would it be for him to be living with an adult who suspects he's from another planet?

If I pursued this, I'd lose my son.

The thought was intolerable. I might never recover. I was sure that he wouldn't. For the first time in his life, he'd finally formed an attachment. What would it do to him to have it broken so abruptly? It would truly destroy his ability to trust any other human being.

I couldn't do that to him. I couldn't do *anything* that might hurt him.

And what about me? I had my own "attachment issues." I couldn't stand the thought of failure. Not here. Not this one.

That was where I stayed stuck for the longest time. I walked around the house in physical pain for three weeks. My chest hurt. My head hurt. My legs hurt. My back hurt. My eyes hurt. My throat hurt. The only part of me that didn't hurt was my brain. That was so numb, I couldn't think. The only time I didn't hurt was when I was stirring a pot of pickled mongoose for breakfast.

See, this is the thing about writing—about being a writer. You have to believe in it first. Because if you don't believe in it, no one else will. So you learn to do the Red Queen's trick, and you practice believing six impossible things before breakfast.*

Little fur balls that breed like crazy. An intelligence engine that asks what it means to be a human being. A time machine in a belt that lets you reedit your own life. A golden starship made out of its own thoughts. A battle-weary crew fighting a never-ending space war. A world where people choose their sex at puberty. Giant, pink man-eating worms from outer space. It's all in the believing.

Give the reader a million pieces of detail and he doesn't question the one detail you don't give him. Wrap the impossible in the probable and it looks inevitable.

And that's what writers do. Yeah, I know we like to dress it up in poetry—that we're turning our imaginations loose to graze in the fields of whimsy and then we follow after with a butterfly net. But that's just more confabulating about the nature of confabulating.

What we do *really*—well, maybe I'm only speaking for myself here—is let go of reality altogether and sail away out of our heads into domains of consciousness that have as much to do with chemical imbalance as anything else. There are no road maps.

To say that a writer's hold on reality is tenuous is an understatement—it's like saying the *Titanic* had a rough crossing. Writers build their own realities, move into them, and occasionally send letters home.

Through the Looking Glass, by Lewis Carroll.

The only difference between a writer and a crazy person is that a writer gets paid for it.

Any sane person would have dismissed the whole thing as wild coincidence—but I don't deal well with coincidence; it's bad plotting. My job is to construct and contrive and pretend that chaos can be edited for meaning. And this time, I had done it so well I had convinced myself that there was meaning here with no compelling evidence at all.

If I put aside the possibility of coincidence, only two possibilities remained: *Either I'm really crazy* or *Dennis really is a Martian*.

Either way, I lose.

If I'm crazy, then I can't be trusted with him.

And if he really is a Martian, then I can't be trusted with him either.

Whichever it is, I can't tell anyone.

I STARTED LOOKING FOR EVIDENCE.

I began browsing through my journal.

I'd been making daily notes of interesting incidents, in case I ever wanted to write a book about our experiences. At first, I couldn't find anything. Most of the incidents I'd writ-

ten about were fairly mundane. Not even good *Readers'*
Digest material.

For instance, the week after he moved in, I'd taken him
to the baseball game at Dodger Stadium. As we pulled into
the parking lot, I said, "Okay, kiddo, wish for a parking place."

Dennis leaned forward in his seat, an intense expression
on his face.

"Looks crowded. Better wish hard."

I came to the end of the row and turned around into the
next one. There were six empty places.

"Whoops. You overdid it."

"I made a Martian wish."

"Oh, okay. Well, there are five people behind us who
need parking places too. Now, let's go see the greatest baseball team in the whole world. You know who that is?"

"The Dodgers!"

"Right!"

For the first part of the game, Dennis was more interested in having a pennant and getting some cotton candy than
in what was going on down on the stadium floor. But along
about the fifth inning, he climbed up onto my lap and I began
explaining the game to him. "See that man at home plate,
holding the bat. Wish for him to hit the ball right out of the
park."

"Okay," said Dennis.

Cra-a-ack! The ball went sailing straight out into the
right field stands. Someone in the lower deck caught it and

the runner sauntered easily around the bases while the organist played, "Glory, Glory, Hallelujah."

"You're a good wisher, Dennis. That was terrific. Want to try it again?"

"No."

"Okay."

Two innings later, the Dodgers were one run behind. I asked Dennis to wish for hits. Four pitches later, there were runners at first and third.

It didn't matter to me who came up to bat now; I hadn't remembered the names of any ballplayers since Roy Campanella was catching for Don Drysdale and Sandy Koufax. As far as I was concerned, Who was on first, What was on second, and I Don't Know still played third. I liked baseball only so long as I didn't have to be an expert; but I'd never seen the Dodgers win a game. Every time I came to the stadium they lost; so I'd made it a point to stay away from Dodger Stadium to give them a fair chance at winning. I didn't expect them to win tonight, but Dennis's wishes had brought them from three runs behind.

"Okay, Dennis," I said, giving him a little squeeze. "It's time for one last wish. See that guy at the home plate, holding the bat? You gotta wish for him to hit a home run. All the way out of the park. Just like before. Okay?"

"Okay."

And just like before—*cra-a-ack*—the ball went sailing deep into right field, triggering a sudden cluster of excited fans scrambling down across the empty seats.

The Dodgers won that night. All the way home, I kept praising Dennis for his excellent wishing.

A couple of weeks after that, we were stopped at a light, waiting for it to change. It was one of those intersections that existed slightly sideways to reality. Whenever you stopped there, time slowed down to a crawl. Without even thinking, I said, "Dennis, wish for the light to turn green, please."

"Okay," he said.

—and abruptly the light turned green. I frowned. It seemed to me the cycle hadn't quite completed.

Nah. I must have been daydreaming. I eased the car through the intersection. A moment later, we got caught at the next red light. I said a word.

"Why'd you say that?"

"These lights are supposed to be synchronized," I said. "So you only get green ones. We must be out of synch. Why don't you wish for this light to change too please."

"Okay."

—green.

"Boy! You are really a good wisher."

"Thank you."

A minute later, I said, "Can you wish this light to turn green too?"

"No," he said, abruptly angry. "You're going to use up all my wishes."

"Huh?" I looked over at him.

"I only have so many wishes and you're going to use them all up on stoplights." There was a hurt quality in his voice.

I turned to him and put my hand gently on his shoulder. "Oh, sweetheart. I don't know who told you that, but that's not so. The wish bag is bottomless. You can have as many wishes as you want."

"No, you can't," he insisted. And then, abruptly, "I wished for my *Ghostbusters* blanket and I never got it!"

"What *Ghostbusters* blanket?"

"When I was living with Pat—" *The one who abused him.* "—I had a *Ghostbusters* blanket, it was my favorite thing in the whole world, whenever I wrapped myself up in it, I felt safe, and she took it away from me, she said I could have it when I moved and then she said no I couldn't, she wouldn't let me take it with, it was my favorite blanket, it was mine, it was the only thing I wanted—" The words came out in an incoherent rush, a sudden torrent of emotion; he broke down in great, heaving sobs. "—it was my blanket! I want my blanket back! I wished for it and I never got it back! She took it away from me and wouldn't let me have it. She was a bitch! A fucking bitch! A dirty, bastard-ass, fucking bitch!"

I was already pulling the car over to the curb. I didn't know where we were, I didn't care. Traffic rushed past in the night, the force of the wind shaking the car almost as much as Dennis's impossible sobs. I pulled him over to me, onto my lap and let him bawl. His whole body was shaking. I'd never seen him like this—

—in fact, I'd never seen him cry at all before this. This was the first time he'd ever let me see what kind of anguish he was carrying around.

And I didn't know what to do.

I couldn't think of anything to say.

A long time ago, I'd learned that if you don't know what to say, but you have to say something, repeat the other person's last statement. At least, that way they know you're listening.

So I echoed his anguish back to him. "I'm so sorry, sweetheart. Your favorite blanket. I bet you felt so safe in it. And she wouldn't let you take it. What a terrible thing to do." Over and over again. "I wish I knew where to get you another *Ghostbusters* blanket. If I could find one for you, I would. Because it means so much to you." But I knew that was insufficient.

"It isn't fair. She was supposed to take good care of me. And she didn't. She got mad and took my blanket and wouldn't let me have it. Fuck her! *Fuck Pat! With a red-hot poker!*" Now he was alternating between racking cries of anguish and screams of astonishing rage.

"This was when you were four? And you're still angry? Wow, that blanket really must have meant a lot to you! What a terrible thing to do to a little kid. I'm so sorry, sweetheart. If that had happened to me, I'd be just as angry as you."

"I want my blanket. It's mine! *Not hers!*"

I glanced at my watch. We'd been doing this for twenty minutes now—isn't it amazing how time flies even when you're not having fun? But this was part of the job too—maybe even the best part. Because this was the part when he needed me the most—and I could be there for him.

But I didn't feel like I was making a difference. No matter what I said, his rage and anguish just kept on coming. Didn't this kid's batteries ever run down?

"Dennis, listen to me. I know that there is no blanket in the world that means as much to you. And you know that if I could get that blanket back for you, I'd do that right now—wherever it is. You know that, don't you?"

He stopped raging long enough to nod into my shirt, wiping his nose on me.

"But I *can* buy you a new blanket. You can pick it out yourself. And I can promise you that no one will ever take this one away. I know it's not the same—but maybe it could be special because I got it for you?"

He nodded, but then he added somberly, "I wished for my blanket and I never got it back."

"Well, maybe only the important wishes come true."

"*None* of my wishes come true—"

Oh? I knew how to flatten that one. "What's the most important thing you ever wished for?"

He didn't answer.

"What's the most important wish?" I repeated.

Very softly, he admitted, "I wished for a dad. Someone who would be nice to me."

"Uh-huh. And did you get your wish?"

He nodded.

"So, you see, sweetheart. There's no shortage of wishes."

"But that was a Martian wish—"

"A Martian wish."

"Uh-huh."

"Oh, well, that's different, then."

"Martian wishes always come true."

"Of course."

I noted the conversation in my journal and let the matter slide. But it left me with an uncomfortable feeling. What has to happen to a child to make him believe there's a limit to wishes?

A year later, I looked at the words I'd written glowing on the computer screen, and wondered about Dennis's ability to wish. It was probably a coincidence. But maybe it wasn't. That time we'd matched four out of six numbers in the lottery and won eighty-eight dollars—was that the week I'd asked him to wish real hard for us to win?

Hmm.

~~~~~~~~~~~~~~~~~~~~~~~~~~~~~~~~

Dennis LIKES CLEANING THINGS. Without asking, he'll go out and wash the car, or the patio. He'll give the dog baths. He'll vacuum the rugs and take the Dustbuster to the couch. He'll mop the floors. His favorite toys are a sponge and a squirt-bottle of Simple Green. Once, he found a rusty old wrench in a vacant field and scrubbed the rust away until it shone like new.

One night after dinner, after he finished methodically loading the dishwasher, I sat him down at the kitchen table and told him I had a surprise for him.

"What?"

"It's a book of puzzles."

"Oh." He sounded disappointed.

"No, listen. Here's the game. You have twenty minutes to do these puzzles. Then when you finish, I add them up and we'll find out how smart you are. Do you want to do this?"

"It'll really tell you how smart I am?"

"Uh-huh."

He grabbed for the book and a pencil.

"Wait a minute—let me set the timer. Okay? Now, once you start, you can't stop. You have to go all the way through to the end. Okay?"

"Okay."

"Ready?"

"Ready."

"One, two, three . . . go."

He attacked the first three puzzles with a vengeance. They were simple. Pick the next shape in a series: triangle, square, pentagon . . . ? Which object doesn't belong: horse, cow, sheep, scissors? *Feather* is to *bird* as *fur* is to: dog, automobile, ice cream . . . ?

Then the puzzles started getting harder and he started to frown. He brushed his hair out of his eyes and once he stopped to clean his glasses; but he stayed interested and involved and when the timer went off, he didn't want to stop. He insisted that he be allowed to finish the puzzle he was working on. What the hell. I let him.

"What does it say?" Dennis asked as I computed the percentile. He wanted to grab the test book out of my hand.

"Well . . . let me finish here." I held it out of his reach as I checked the table of percentiles.

The test showed that he had above-average intelligence—not unexpected; hyperactive kids tend to be brighter than average—but well within the normal range for a nine-year-old. "It says that you are fifty-two inches high, that you weigh sixty-six pounds, and that your daddy loves you very much. It also says that you are very smart."

"How smart?"

"Well, if this test were given to one hundred children, you would be smarter than ninety-two of them."

"How good is that?"

"That's *very* good. You can't get much better. And it means we should go out for ice cream after dinner. What do you think?"

"Yeah!"

Oh, that was another thing. He didn't like chocolate. He preferred rainbow sherbet. I'd never seen that in a kid before.

No *chocolate?*

A COUPLE OF WEEKS LATER, WE played another game. I made sure to pick a quiet evening, one with no distractions. I cleared everything off the table, leaving only a candy bowl of M&M's.

"This game is even harder," I explained. "It's a guessing game," I explained. "See these cards? There are six different shapes here. A circle, a square, a star, three squiggly lines, a cross, and a figure-eight. All you have to do is guess which one I'm looking at. See if you can read my mind, okay?"

He frowned at me, and I had to explain it two or three more times. This was not a game he wanted to play. I said okay and started to put the deck away. If he didn't want to cooperate, the results would be inconclusive. "Can we go for ice cream after we do this?" he asked abruptly.

"Sure," I said.

"Okay, let's do it."

"We have to do it five times. Do you think you can do it that many times?"

He shrugged.

I laid out a paper in front of him, showing him the shapes so he would be able to remember them all. I told him he could close his eyes if it would help him concentrate. Instead, he leaned forward and stared intently at me.

I began turning cards over. I did it slowly, looking at each one in turn, thinking each shape to myself without regard for anything else.

Dennis stared into my eyes and began calling out shapes. "Star. Circle. Circle. Wavy lines. Box. Star. Box."

I stopped.

Every guess had been right.

I stared across the table at him. He looked very proud of himself. "I got 'em right, didn't I?"

I nodded slowly. "How did you do that?"

He smiled shyly and admitted, "I looked at the reflection in your glasses."

"Okay," I said. I had to admire his ingenuity. "You want to try it again? This time, we'll cover your eyes. I have a blindfold for sleeping on an airplane, that should work—"

"Wavy lines. Box. Star. Circle. Wavy lines. Star. Star. Box—"

Whew. Martians aren't telepathic. This was very good news. I wasn't sure I wanted to live with a telepathic child.

"—Box. Lines. Circle. Circle. Star. Lines. Star. Red. Yellow. Yellow. Orange. Green . . ."

Huh? I looked up from the deck. Blindfolded, Dennis was popping M&M's into his mouth, one at a time. He would hold it between his fingers—there was no way he could see through the blindfold—then put it on his tongue, taste it for a second, and announce the color.

125

And every guess was *right*. Except they weren't guesses, were they?

Martians can taste colors?

"Brown. Orange. Red. Yellow. Brown. Green . . ."

I opened my briefcase. The Mars company had just retired tan candies in favor of blue ones. I had purchased a large bag. I opened it now and poured some of them into the candy bowl. *Wow*—blue M&M's!

". . . Yellow, green—*yick!* What was that?" Dennis spit the candy into his hand and pulled off the blindfold. *"Blue?"* He looked betrayed.

"It's a new color. Don't you like it?"

He made a face. "No." And then he added, "It tastes like pickled mongoose."

That felt like a good place to stop. I started gathering up the cards.

"Are we done? Who won the game?"

"Franz Kafka. Come on, let's go get some ice cream."

"Who's Frank Zafka?"

"Just some writer who went buggy."

"Really buggy?"

"Yep. And I know exactly how he felt."

So, Martians weren't telepathic.

But they can taste colors.

Maybe that's why they like rainbow sherbet so much.

THERE WERE OTHER TESTS. NOT many. Not anything too weird. Just little ones that might indicate if there was something worth further investigation. There wasn't. As near as I could determine, there was nothing so unusual about Dennis that it would register as a statistical anomaly in a repeatable, testable circumstance. He couldn't levitate. He couldn't move objects. He couldn't make things disappear. He didn't know how to *grok*. He could only hold his breath for thirty-three seconds. He couldn't *think* muscles. He couldn't see around corners.

But—

He *could* predict elevators. Take him into any building, anywhere. Take him to the elevator bank. Let him push the *up* button. Don't say a word. Without fail, the door he stands in front of will be the one where the first elevator arrives. Was he wishing them or predicting them? I don't know. It's useful only at science fiction conventions, which are legendary for recalcitrant elevators. It has little value anywhere else in the world.

He could make stop lights turn green—sometimes. Mostly, he waited until he saw the lights for the cross street turn yellow before he announced his wish. Maybe he could still make the Dodgers score four runs in two innings—but it wasn't consistent. We went back to Dodger Stadium in May, and either Dennis wasn't wishing or he really had used up all his wishes.

He *could* sing with perfect pitch, especially if the lyrics were about Popeye's gastrointestinal distress. He could play a video game for four hours straight without food or water. He could invent an amazing number of excuses for not staying in bed. He could also hug my neck so hard that once I felt a warning crack in my trachea. My throat hurt for a week afterward.

I began to think that *maybe* I had imagined the whole thing.

And that would have been just fine with me.

On school nights, I tucked him in at nine-thirty. We had a whole ritual. If there was time, we read a storybook together; whatever was appropriate. Afterward, prayers—

"I'm sorry God for . . . I didn't do anything to be sorry for."

"How about sassing your dad? Remember you had to take a time-out?"

"Oh, yeah. I'm sorry God, for sassing my dad. Thank you God for . . . um, I can't think of anything."

"Going swimming?"

"No. Thank you God for Calvin, my cat."

"Good. Anything else you want to say to God?"

"Does God hear the prayers of Martians?"

"Uh . . . of course he does. God hears everybody's prayers."

"Not Martians."

"Yes, even Martians."

"Uh-uh."

"Why do you say no?"

"Because God didn't make any Martians."

"If God didn't make the Martians, then who did?"

"The devil."

"Did the devil make you?"

"Uh-huh."

"How do you know?"

"Because . . . I'm a Martian."

I remembered a little speech I'd made just about a year ago. *Let it be all right for him to be a Martian for as long as he needs to be.* "All right," I said. "But let me tell you a secret," I whispered. "The devil didn't make any Martians. That's just a lie the devil wants you to believe. God made the Martians."

"Really?"

"Cross my heart and hope to die. Stick a noodle in my eye."

"How do you know?" He was very insistent.

"Because I talk to God every night," I said. "Just like you, I say my prayers. And God made everything in the world."

"But Martians aren't from this world—"

"That's right. But God made Mars too. And everything on it. Just like she made this world, she made a whole bunch of others, and Mars was one of them. Honest."

"How come you say *she* when you talk about God?"

"Because sometimes God is female and sometimes God is male. God is everything. And now it's time for you to stop asking questions and go to sleep. Hugs and kisses?"

"Hugs and kisses."

"G'night. No more talking."

"I love you."

"I love you too. Now no more talking."

"Dad?" he called me back.

"What?"

"I have to tell you something."

"What?"

"I love you."

"I love you too. Now, *shhh*. No more talking, Dennis."

"G'night."

"Sleep tight—"

Finally, I got smart. I stopped answering. Control freaks. We each wanted to have the last word.

I PADDED BAREFOOT DOWN THE HALL. I stopped in the living room long enough to turn off the television set, the VCR, the surround-sound system, all the little robots of mindless entertainment. I continued on through the dining room and finally to my office. Two computers sat on my desk, both showing that it was 9:47. The monster-child had manipulated an extra seventeen minutes tonight.

I sat down in my chair, leaned back, put my feet up on my desk, and stared out at the dark waters of the swimming pool in the backyard. The pool glowed with soft, blue light. The night was . . . silent. Somewhere, our dog, mumbled to himself.

Almost every night, just as Dennis began saying his prayers, Somewhere would come ambling down the hall, a big, shaggy, absentminded canine-American. He'd step over everything that was in his way, uncaring if he knocked over a day's worth of Lego construction. He'd climb onto the bed, over my lap, over Dennis, grumbling softly as he found his position next to Dennis. The day that Dennis moved in, Somewhere had changed his sleeping route to include the new "puppy." With his prehensile tongue, he could slurp the inside of Dennis's right ear from the left side of his head, taking either the internal or external route.

Tonight, though, he knew I wasn't finished working. I had some serious thinking to do, so he joined me in the office, taking his station under the desk, and sighing about the overtime. "You're in super-golden hours," I reminded him; he shut up.

Whenever I'm in doubt about something, I sit down and start writing. I write down everything I'm feeling or thinking or worrying about. I say everything there is to say until there's nothing left to say. The first time I did this was the day after my father died. I sat and wrote for two days. When I was finished, I had a story called "In the Deadlands." I never did figure out what it was about, but it still gives me the shudders.

But I learned something from that experience—maybe the most important thing I've ever learned about storytelling. Effective writing isn't in the mechanics. Anyone can master the mechanical act of stringing together words and sentences and paragraphs to make a character move from *A* to *B*. The bookstores are full of evidence. But that's not writing. Writing isn't about words, it's about experience. It's about the *feeling* that the story creates inside of you. If there's no feeling, there's no story.

But sometimes, there's only the feeling without any meaning or understanding. And that's not a story either. What I was feeling about Dennis was so confusing and troubling and uncertain that I couldn't even begin to sort it out. I needed to write down all the separate pieces—as if in the act of telling, it would sort itself out. Sometimes the process worked.

And sometimes it was a trap. The thing about writing is that sometimes you believe in stuff so completely that you *can't* stop believing in it. And then you're stuck with whatever you created. Whether it's pickled mongoose or silly faces or Martian wishes.

Maybe I was believing too hard.

Maybe I was just an idiot.

Certainly, the universe seems to enjoy reminding me of that fact.

When I looked up again, three hours had passed. My back and shoulders ached. The dog had gone to bed, and I felt I had accomplished nothing at all except to delineate the scale of my frustration.

Why would an alien species come to this planet? The last time I spent that much time on this question, I came up with giant, pink man-eating slugs in search of new flavors. But why would Martians send their children to Earth?

The most logical idea I could come up with was that they were here as observers. Spies.

Have you ever been pulling on your underwear and realized that your dog or your cat is watching you? Have you ever considered the possibility that the creature is sharing your secrets with some clandestine network of dogs and cats? *"Oh, you think that's weird? My human wears underwear with pictures of Rocky and Bullwinkle on them."*

But dogs and cats are limited in what they can observe. If you *really* want to know a culture, you have to be a member of it. But an alien couldn't step in and pretend to be a member of this culture, could he? He'd have to learn. He'd have to be taught. . . .

Where could a Martian go to get lessons in being a human? Who gives lessons in human beingness?

Mommies and Daddies. That's right.

~~~~~~~~~~~~~~~~~~~~~~~~~~~~~~~~~~~~~~~

K ATHY BRIGHT HAD GIVEN ME SEVeral huge stacks of reports on Dennis, written by various therapists and counselors. I hadn't had time to read them all, and after the first few, I stopped—I didn't want *their* experience of Dennis; I wanted to make up my own mind.

But as I paged through the files, looking to see if there was any Martian stuff, one of them caught my eye. On Saturday, June 27, 1992, Carolyn Green (the counselor on his case at the time) had noted, *"Dennis thinks God doesn't hear his prayers, because he wished for a dad and nothing happened."*

I first saw Dennis's picture on Saturday, June 27, 1992, at about two in the afternoon. According to Carolyn Green's report, that was the exact time of his weekly session. I cannot help but believe that he was wishing for a dad at the exact moment I first saw his picture. *A Martian wish.* Was that what I felt so strongly?

I LOOKED UP FROM THE STACK OF
paper, and there he was, staring at me, eyes wide—almost in
fear.

"What's the matter?" I asked, suddenly concerned.

"I couldn't sleep. You woke me up."

"I'm sorry—" Except I hadn't been making any noise at
all. I'd been hunched over a stack of papers for the last half
hour, reading and frowning and scratching my ear. I hadn't
realized that ear-scratching was so loud.

"Come on, sweetheart." I picked him up. I liked picking
him up. I liked holding him and feeling his little arms slide
around my neck in a familiar hug. I liked this kid. I liked the
way his hair smelled of shampoo and the way he felt *right* in
my arms. I carried him back to his bed. "I'll tuck you back in."

"Daddy?"

"Yes, son?"

"Are you unhappy about something?"

"Not really. I was just trying to figure something out.
That's all."

"What?"

"How much I love you, that's what."

"I don't want you to be unhappy."

135

"I'm not unhappy."

He wasn't satisfied. "Daddy, I wish for you to be happy."

I had to smile. I laid him down in his bed. "Was that a Martian wish?" I asked.

"Yes," he said, in a voice that left no room for disagreement.

"Then, I'm happy," I said. And in fact, I was.

I hadn't realized it before, because I hadn't acknowledged it, not even to myself; but as I walked back down the hall to my office, I had to admit I was glowing.

I'd gotten everything I'd wanted, a wonderful son, a profound sense of family, a whole new reason for waking up in the morning. So what if he's a Martian, it really doesn't matter, does it?

He's my *son*, and I love him. And I'm happy.

~~~~~~~~~~~~~~~~~

AND THEN . . . *NOTHING WEIRD happened.*

Life went on.

One day, Michael Brown asked about Dennis.

I said, "He's starting to relax and get used to the idea he's in a family."

Michael grinned and said, "So are you."

"It shows, huh?"

"Yep."

And then it was January again.

~ ~ ~ ~ ~ ~ ~ ~ ~ ~ ~ ~ ~ ~ ~ ~

IMAGINE THE WORST AIRPLANE TUR-
bulence you've ever been in. Now imagine worse than that.
Imagine the plane bouncing around so hard that the pilot has
everyone in the crash position. Imagine the flight attendants
crying. Imagine things flying and crashing and bouncing
around the cabin. Now imagine it *in the dark*.

Now imagine it's your house that's doing it.

Imagine all the panic you've ever felt in your entire life
forcing itself out through your throat in the space of half a
second—screaming out of you before you even know what's
happening, the whole world rolling up and down in grinding
waves of terror.

Imagine the ground screaming like a vertical freight train
roaring up out of the darkness beneath you. And then the
crashing begins, the sound of everything you own; bouncing,
jumping, breaking, flinging itself back and forth across the
rooms of your house.

4:31 in the morning. Hanging onto the bed. Listening to the world crash. Green flashes of lightning, one, two, three, forever—as all the electrical transformers in the alley crackled and exploded, one after the other. The water from the pool came splashing against the window of my bedroom—

And then silence. Darkness, total. The awful pause of anticipation—hesitation and paralysis. My God! What now?

"Dennis, are you all right?" His room, across from mine; I couldn't get there, something was blocking my door, the big bookshelf at the end of the hall had fallen against it, stuff all over the floors, I pulled the door open, climbed over the mess, picked my way to *my son* as fast as I could—grabbed him, held him tight, held him close forever. "Are you all right, sweetheart?"

"You woke me up—"

"We had an earthquake. Didn't you feel it? Are you all right? Nothing fell on you?"

"Nuh-uh."

"Okay, good, good. That's all that matters."

I'd planned his room to be earthquake safe, the bed over here by the structural walls, the bookshelves *over there* in the opposite corner, so nothing could fall on him. But even though I knew, I didn't *know*.

I ran my hands over him, his head, his shoulders, his back, checking him in the dark, reassuring myself that he was unharmed. Then I grabbed him and held him close—and held him and held him, terrified—not of the earthquake anymore, but that he might have been so scared he couldn't stand it. The earth had just stolen my sense of well-being. What had it taken from him?

Somewhere in the confusion, I remembered Somewhere. The thought came up like questions—didn't we have a dog? Where was he? Oh, no—if anything ever happened to the pooch—

"*Somewhere?* Where are you?"

Almost immediately, I heard the sound of scrabbling dog claws on a hardwood floor. He was under the headboard of my bed. He must have scrambled there at the first jolt—that's where he always hid during thunderstorms—at least, when he couldn't hide under my pillow—

"All right," I called. "You stay there, pooch. Just stay." For the first time in his life, the dog obeyed. Usually, one word from me and he did exactly what he wanted. But this time, maybe he was too scared. "Dennis, stay right here in bed for a minute. Don't move."

A flashlight—I knew I had a flashlight somewhere. I'd been putting together earthquake boxes for twenty years. Now if I could only find one. The problem was, Dennis liked flashlights, so he was always taking them and playing with them and losing them—I bought flashlights every two weeks. There must be a working one somewhere in this house. If I could find it. But there were books and videotapes and CDs everywhere, everything I owned was on the floor, and I had to pick my way through it in the dark.

My neighbor from across the street pushed open my

front door, shouting in: "David? Are you all right?" I could see the beam of his light playing around the living room.

"Yeah, yeah, we're all right—let me borrow your flashlight for a minute, so I can find my own—"

I padded near-naked through the house, picking my way through assorted messes, listening to my own astonishment— "Oh, God. Oh, no. Oh, damn. Oh, hell. Oh, *shit!*" Punctuated by the even more annoyed realization: *Wow, what great source material!* Followed by my own reaction: *Sheesh, don't you ever stop? No, why should I? Oh, God. Help me out here. I'm trapped inside a self-aware writer.* The whole conversation lasted half a second. Then, I got serious.

First, find Dennis's meds. The Ritalin. The Clonodine. We'd just refilled the prescription. I'd put the bags right *here* on the big shelf of CDs where they would be convenient— the shelf that had flung itself across the dining room, leaving five hundred compact discs scattered like the dead leaves of January. The pills were—*here!* Okay, good. Dennis was safe, the dog was safe, we had the meds. We had bottled water. We had—no electricity, but that was okay, the food in the fridge would stay cold for a while. We had milk and bread and cereal. We'd done a big shopping only two days ago—

I aimed the flashlight into the kitchen.

Oh, shit.

Broken glass, spaghetti sauce, leftover stir-fry, ketchup, relish, mustard, pancake batter, maple syrup, cream sherry, beer, steak sauce, homemade soup, frozen peas, milk, breakfast cereal, all generously topped with every spice from curry powder to chili. The shelves were bare. Every dish was broken on the floor. Every mug. Every glass. Everything. The kitchen would have to be cleaned with a shovel.

My office—I couldn't get very far into it—three huge lateral filing cabinets had danced across the floor, blocking the hall. I didn't know if either of the computers had survived; I'd backed up one to the other only two days before, so if either hard disk had survived, I was still in business. My 21" monitor was *not* on my desk—

I pushed open the back door and looked out at the yard. The water in the pool—the water that had *stayed* in the pool—was still sloshing angrily back and forth. And as if to add insult to injury, that's when the first aftershock hit— bringing down the brick wall, toppling it sideways, flattening three years of gardening, and filling the pool with concrete blocks.

I got Dennis dressed and we spent the next hour on the street in front of the house, standing around with all the neighbors. It was dark and it was cold and there was a pink glow in the sky to the northeast. Something was on fire.

The phones were out, of course, but I tried my cell phone. The only number I could remember was my editor in New York. I phoned and left a message on her answering machine. "We've had an earthquake, it's pretty bad, but Dennis and I are all right. The phones are likely to be out for a while, so please call around and let folks know." That was the only call I was able to make. A few minutes later, the cell phone network stopped responding too. They shut the

networks down so that they're available for emergency use—
yeah, right. If they shut them down, how are we supposed to
use them for emergency calls?

There was nothing else we could do, except wait for
dawn. We were going to have a lot of work to do. Already I
was thinking about insurance and cleaning and rebuilding,
and groaning inside. This was not the way I had planned to
spend the next year of my life.

Finally, I took Dennis back into the house, wrapped him
up in a blanket and put him down on one end of the living
room couch. I grabbed another blanket for myself and curled
up on the other end.

~~~~~~~~~~~~~~~~~~~~~~~~

DANIEL KEYS MORAN DROVE IN
from San Bernardino with a car full of bread, milk, fresh eggs,
salad, fruit, vegetables, and even a portable generator. It was
a three-hour drive; two of the local freeways were closed until
Cal-Trans could check all the overpasses. And Todd McCaf-
frey, Anne's number-two son, came by with a shovel and
cleaned out the kitchen. He and Dan picked up the books
and the CDs for me—later, they told me I had looked like a
zombie. Dan said he'd never seen so many people in one
place, all looking as if they had just been beaten up.

I kept telling myself to take it one day at a time. Just do what's next.

The pool service man came out, looked at the pool, groaned, shook his head, went away . . .

We drained the pool—I hired some guys and they began pulling the bricks out of the pool, dumping them in a pile in front of the house—and then all the rest of the bricks that had once been a wall. Eventually, there was a barricade of bricks so high that the neighbors across the street thought I was preparing for war. I wasn't the only one. Wherever you went, there were long piles of bricks that had previously been walls. The city looked like a war zone.

Without power, we had no television, and I couldn't listen to the car radio for more than two minutes at a time—my attention span had been destroyed. So, for a couple of days, I assumed that this had been *the big one*—that the whole city had been leveled.

Later, I found out we had been riding the epicenter. Literally. The map in the newspaper had an arrow pointing to our house.

The San Fernando Valley had been lifted up and dropped *twelve feet*. Then the rest of the quake began. . . . The whole basin rang like a bell that had been struck with a sledgehammer. It was like being punched awake. It was like being kicked out of bed so you could be pummeled. This quake had a personality—it was *vicious*.

According to the map, the only way we could have gotten closer to the thrust fault, we would have had to go underground. The earthquake had been centered under my waterbed—I am not making this up. Thanks a lot, God. I already have enough source material. Isn't Dennis enough? What else do you have in store for me?

Very quickly, I found out—

The earth did not want to settle. Every day we still got window-rattling *thumps*, loud enough to bring me shouting out of my chair. "Goddammit! Enough already!" And I'd stamp my foot as if to punish the jelly-belly ground. "No more shaking!" After I stamped my foot enough times, the Earth would quiet down. It always worked. At least, until the next aftershock.

Dennis's initial exuberance and excitement had faded into sullenness. He'd spent Saturday organizing his room all nice and neat. The earthquake had undone everything. He didn't want to pick it all up again—not until one of my students from Pepperdine came out and the two of them worked on it together for a day. But all of the other damage to the house— the pool, the chimney, the kitchen, the wall around the yard, the deep cracks in all the walls, the broken bookshelves, the loss of every breakable thing we had, every glass, every dish— had taken its toll. His feeling of safety had been broken—and maybe this time for keeps. After all, if you couldn't trust the very earth under your feet, who could you trust?

About a week after the quake, Dennis came to me, as apologetic as I'd ever seen him. "Daddy, I'm sorry—"

"For what?"

"I knew we were going to have an earthquake. I forgot to tell you."

I went down on one knee and gathered him into a hug. "No, sweetheart—don't do that. Nobody knows when an earthquake is going to happen. That's why we have to be prepared all the time. That's why we put the shelves away from your bed, that's why we had three emergency boxes. That's why we have smoke alarms and bottled water and everything else."

"But I knew—" he insisted.

"No, sweetheart. Nobody knows. Nobody. But everybody is always talking about earthquake preparedness, just in case. You do not get to blame yourself. Promise me that."

"Okay."

"Promise?"

"Okay."

"Is that a real promise?"

"Okay."

I knew he didn't believe me.

Three weeks later, we were walking home from McDonald's. We still hadn't started cooking again. We hadn't even bought new dishes yet. He asked, "Daddy? What causes earthquakes?"

"Plate tectonics," I answered, hoping I wouldn't have to explain plate tectonics.

He considered that carefully. We walked a little further. Then, abruptly, he shouted angrily, *"Fuck plate tectonics!"*

I nodded in agreement. I put my arm around him and pulled him close. "Hey, it's just stuff, and we can always get more stuff. The important thing is that you and me and

Somewhere are all okay. We're a team, and we're bigger than any problem, right?"

"Right."

I hoped that would be good enough.

And then one night, we came home from dinner at Grandma's—

Grandma Jo and Grandpa Harvey had missed the earthquake. They were on a cruise in the Caribbean. Thank God. The earthquake had collapsed a large part of their apartment building. Their apartment had survived, sort of. Except it now sagged with a decidedly southward tilt. We had twenty-four hours to get all their furniture out before it was officially condemned. My stepbrother hired a moving company and the two of us, plus a couple of nephews, went over to pack up what we could. It was two days after the quake and the aftershocks were coming like birth contractions. I went into my mother's sewing room and packed up all her photo albums. Everyone and everything she'd ever loved was remembered in those big books—everything else was replaceable, but not the photo albums. By the time they got back, my sister had found a condo for them to sublet, so they came out of the quake in better shape than most folks.

So we ate dinner over there a lot. It was comfort food and reassurance.

But this night—

—I walked in the front door, Dennis following. Somewhere was snoozing on the couch. He didn't get up. I headed for the kitchen—

"Daddy, there's something wrong with Somewhere!"

—It was as if my legs had been kicked out from under me—my buddy, my pal, my writing partner, my footstool, my pickle-nose-pooch, my canine brother—he was limp, warm, but lifeless—no pulse, no eye reaction, no muscle reaction—I lifted up his tail. His anus was relaxed, absolute evidence—I gathered him in my arms and sobbed into his shaggy body; he was already gone.

"He's dead." I gulped the words out. And *I hadn't been here for him*—

Dennis backed away, screaming. Terrified. He wouldn't come near. I scooped him up and carried him to his bedroom. *Oof.* This kid was getting heavy. I grabbed his new Batman comforter and wrapped him up in it like a burrito.

At first he tried to fight me away, but I wouldn't let go. I held him close on my lap and rocked him in my arms while he raged and screamed and sobbed. Neither of us got any sleep that night. He held onto me and we cried together for a long, long time, punctuated only by his insistent questions that I couldn't answer. "I don't know what happened, sweetheart. I don't know."

Dr. Brown did an autopsy. He said it was anaphylactic shock. A bee sting. Or a spider bite. The earthquake had brought a lot of dust and insects up out of the ground. There was an epidemic of spider bites and fungus infections and other weird things—

Explanations are useless. Explanations do not change facts. They do not make facts better. Explanations are the booby prize. You can have all the explanations you want in the world. They do not change what's so.

Somewhere was gone. That was the fact, the rest was words. And life was a lot emptier.

We had a funeral. We buried Somewhere's ashes in the backyard in his favorite place for sunning himself. Dennis's godparents came and we said a nice prayer. We acknowledged what a good pooch Somewhere had been and then we tossed a dog biscuit in with the ashes—nobody should have to go to the next world without taking a little lunch.

It was a good funeral. But Dennis stood blank-faced and closed. He wasn't here anymore.

T HINGS WERE DIFFERENT NOW.

Sullen.

Despite my declaration that we could survive anything, that we were a team, that we were bigger than any problem the universe could throw at us—I was beginning to doubt.

Dennis was acting out more than ever. He disobeyed, he argued, he rebelled in public—at the supermarket, in restaurants, anywhere he wanted something. If he didn't get what he wanted, he made a scene. He made sure I knew that the cost of not letting him have his way would be a tantrum.

He was still stealing things. Not just the loose change from my money jar, not just the parking meter money from the car, but every so often twenty or forty dollars would disappear from my wallet—and Dennis would have a new toy that some neighbor had conveniently given him. And despite repeated confiscations and consequences—he kept it up. Three times he "bought" Walkie-talkies from the local drugstore.

He broke things. My 300-dollar headphones got broken, then my 100-dollar headphones. Three cordless telephones, two portable stereos, a portable cassette recorder—and two important cassettes of notes that I had dictated but not yet transcribed, a VCR, a portable television . . . the list was endless. If it was important to me, it got broken. If it was valuable, it got broken. If it was mine, he assumed it was also his—little trinkets with wonderful memories attached, a collectible glass sculpture worth a thousand dollars, a glass guest of honor trophy, several plaques and pictures.

He played with matches. He climbed out of his window after he was supposed to go to sleep, and went walking around the neighborhood. He got caught shoplifting at the local drugstore. (The manager understood the situation and didn't press charges.)

The suspensions from school were piling up. Even the special education teachers and aides couldn't control him. He was playing the monster-child game. Not giving him a quarter for a video game could result in a ruined evening and two days of chest pains.

The first year and a half had been good. We'd had fun together. But now, it felt like the most important part of all—the relationship—was falling apart.

~~~~~~~~~~~~~~~~~~~~~~~~~~~~~~~~~~~

Too late, I realized that we were in a battle for control.

As long as he refused to be controlled, he was winning. It was the only victory he knew, so it was the only victory he pursued.

I could see the incoming arguments arcing in toward me like mortar shells. Nothing I said or did could keep them from exploding all around me.

Some of the arguments and accusations were irrelevant. Some were uncomfortable. But a couple of them *hurt*.

"It's your fault I'm not going to have a mom! I wanted a mom, and now I'm never going to have one. Because you're gay!"

Yes, he'd said it in anger, but the uncomfortable fact about anger is that it reveals the truth. An angry person says what he's *really* feeling.

"No, you're not going to have a mom. But maybe some-day you'll have a second dad—"

"And you'll love him more than you love me!"

Oh.

"No, sweetheart, I won't. I'm not going to let anyone in my life unless they love you as much as I do. I promise you that. You're more important to me than anyone."

Maybe that was all he wanted to hear. Maybe that was the end of it. And maybe it was only the tip of the iceberg. Somehow the big arguments resolved a lot easier than the little ones. The little battles were never-ending.

The supermarket, for instance, was a major battle-ground. Dennis had to push the cart. Except he didn't push the cart. He rode it. He aimed it. He barreled through the aisles on it. It wasn't a cart—it was a NASCAR racer, a jet fighter, a rocket sled. He was always taking it off on expeditions for cookies and cereal. I would end up searching all over the store for him, my arms full of melting this and much-too-heavy that. In self-defense, I carried a hand-basket.

More than once, I would stop him and explain patiently that the cart had to stay with me. The cart wasn't a toy. The whole purpose of the cart was so that I could put things into it.

"Well, I'm putting things into it too!"

"Not unless I say so—now, you either stay with me, or we're going home."

"You said I could push the cart."

"Listen, kiddo—listen carefully. We are going to do this my way or not at all."

"Why?" he demanded.

"Because I'm the daddy, that's why." *Ooh, that felt good to say.*

"That's not fair!"

"Yes, it is. Because I'm the daddy, I get to make the rules. When you get to be a daddy, you get to make the rules. And your little boy will tell you that you're not fair."

"I'm never going to treat my little boy mean."

"Yeah, I used to say the same thing."

And so it went. Up one aisle and down the next. Without asking, Dennis would start grabbing things off the shelves. "Oh, we gotta buy a pizza slicer. Daddy, buy some beer—I never see you drink beer. Can we buy some cake mix? We need this for the car, so I can clean the vinyl—"

"Dennis, I told you that we're only going to buy what we need *today*—"

"But we *need* this—" A package of steel wool. We already had enough scrubbers to scour Dracula's castle.

"No. We don't. We don't need it today. I cannot afford to buy everything you see. We are on a budget. Do you know what a budget is?"

"But we're rich! We have all those credit cards—"

The doctor said my headaches were caused by too much strain on my eye muscles—I had to stop rolling them heavenward so much.

"Dennis! Stop putting things in the cart!"

"I want to help."

"You can help me most by calming down and following directions." I took him by the shoulders and looked him straight in the eye. "Listen to me. You will stop it right now, or we are going home."

"You don't control me," he said.

Even before I responded, I knew we were going to have a scene. I felt trapped in the conversation. "Yes, I do. *I'm the daddy*. You're the little boy. And you will do what I tell you because that's the way it works."

Dennis turned around and grabbed a box of something from the shelf—he didn't even look to see what it was—and jammed it into the cart.

Calmly, deliberately, I reached into the cart, took out the box of tampons, and put them back on the shelf. "No."

When I turned back to the cart, Dennis pushed me away, grabbed it, and ran down the aisle. "Well, I'm going to push the cart. It's my job—"

People were looking at us now. I didn't care. *"Dennis!"* I chased after him. "I can't put things in the cart if you keep running away—"

But he was already charging off again.

"Martians!" I muttered. Because the word I wanted to say was illegal on this planet.

Of course, no supermarket scene is ever complete without a punchline. Somebody tapped me on the shoulder. I whirled around to see a sweet, little old blue-haired lady with a beatific smile—like she'd just stepped out of a Hallmark commercial. "You need a psychiatrist," she told me. As if she were giving me a precious gift.

I do a fairly reasonable Jack Nicholson impersonation—

halfway between *One Flew Over the Cuckoo's Nest* and *The Shining*. I leered at her insanely and said, "Yeah? What was your first clue?" It was worth it to see the blood drain from her face. People who invite themselves unwanted into my movie get to be comic relief. Or crew members in red shirts. My choice.

Eventually, we made it to the checkout counter—always the most dangerous part of the adventure. Because this was where I would find out about all the other things I was buying—more cookies, candy, a toy, chewing gum, weird cleaning supplies—I put them all aside and told the checker not to ring them up. She knew me, she knew Dennis, she knew the drill.

Dennis started to protest—of course—and without even looking at him, I gave him the stock response: "What part of *no* didn't you understand?"

And then there was the *other* problem—wherever I needed to stand, Dennis always pushed himself in front of me. It was something he'd learned in the group home, where everything was a dominance game—the kids always pushed in front of each other, so Dennis always pushed in front of me. He was responding to me not as an adult, but as another kid he was in competition with. For a while, I had let him get away with it, because I didn't realize what was happening—at least, not until I started to get annoyed. If I had to buy tickets for the movie, he pushed up to the ticket window first; if I had to unlock the front door, he stopped directly in front of the lock. If I went to brush my teeth, he had to use the sink. If I had to go to the bathroom—

And here too, buying groceries, he pushed in ahead of me, so I couldn't get to the little machine to run my card—I had begun physically lifting him up and putting him to one side, saying firmly, *"Don't stand in the way."* It was the only way to train him. Sooner or later, he would get the point—but not before all of Northridge became convinced that I was an abusive and unloving dad. Maybe I needed a T-shirt that said, *Caution: Contents Under Pressure. Inflammable.*

I was discovering—very unpleasantly—that I had a temper. A worse temper than either of my parents had ever displayed.

And today—

I opened my wallet to pay for the groceries. And stopped.

There was no cash in my wallet.

This was going to get ugly. *Very* ugly. I couldn't see any way out.

I turned to my son. "Dennis," I said in that controlled jaw-clenched tone that passes for calm when I've actually lost all self-control. "I had two hundred dollars in here. Ten twenty-dollar bills that I took out of the bank last night. That was our eating money for this week."

He started shouting immediately. "I didn't take it! I didn't do it! Why are you always accusing me?"

"Dennis, we don't have time for a performance of abused orphan. I need the money. Where is it?"

"I didn't take your money! I didn't do it! This is just like the group home where everybody accused me of everything! I didn't do it! Everybody always blames me!"

"Nobody else lives with us, Dennis—" People were star-ing. The entire store. I wanted to open up a hole in space, crawl in and die. I took a breath. I turned to the checker. "I'm sorry. I have a bigger problem to deal with right now. Would you put these aside for me? I have to go to the bank. I'll be back later."

She nodded politely, grimly. We'd had this conversation before. She wasn't the only person in the neighborhood whom I'd had to debrief.

I dragged Dennis out of the store. He was headed toward Richter 9.9. "You always blame me for everything! You never give me a chance!"

"That's right, I never give you a chance. I'm a dreadful human being. I'm a rotten father. I beat you with whips and chains, and make you eat gruel. And I'm about to get even worse than that. No television. No bicycle. No Nintendo. And you're grounded until you're forty."

The tantrum lasted all the way home—getting louder as we approached the imagined sanctuary of the house—and his room. I wasn't looking forward to the next part, either. The shouting, kicking, stamping, door-slamming, drawer-banging, toy-flinging, accompanied by a raging torrent of language so appalling that the very fabric of the universe was in danger of shredding.

This was going to require . . . *Plan 9*.

The one thing I swore I'd never do.

I followed him into his room and snatched him out of the air before he could kick another hole in the bedroom wall.

"Leave me alone! Leave me alone! Let me go! Let me

go!" I wrapped him in a basket hug, a restraining hug, and sat down with him on his bed. He could rage all he wanted now—within the safety of my arms. But he couldn't get out—

And rage he did—

He breathed fire. He called down curses. He pulled down the pillars of the temple, bringing great stone blocks crashing down upon my head. He invoked the seventh circle of Hell. He screamed the Secret Name of the Sevagram. And when that didn't work, he even threatened to call his caseworker.

I peered over his shoulder at my watch. The longest we'd ever gone had been forty-five minutes—I wondered if we were going to break the record this time.

"Are you through?" I asked.

No, he wasn't. He raged for another half century.

"Are you through yet?" I asked again.

No. Still not yet.

"I don't want to live here anymore. I'm calling my caseworker. This is child abuse!"

"No, this is *not* child abuse," I said calmly, not releasing my grip on him. "This is what we do *instead* of child abuse."

"Stop making fun of me! Let me go! Let me go!"

I was starting to get annoyed. I glanced at my watch. Not quite as long as an Oscar broadcast yet, but we were getting there. "You want child abuse? I'll give you child abuse."

"Let me go!"

"You're not giving me any choice, kiddo—" I cleared my throat . . . and began singing: *"It's a small world, after all—"*

"Stop it! Stop it!"

"Are you going to calm down?" He didn't answer. *"It's a world of laughter, a world of tears—"*

"Daddy!!!"

Ah, that was progress.

"Stop it! Stop singing at me!" He went limp. He was ready to cry now. I relaxed my grip, but I didn't quite let go. Now I was comforting, not restraining. Dennis curled up in a fetal position in my lap, whimpering softly. I began stroking his head and back, long, calming strokes. "You can test me all you want," I whispered. "But I am *not* quitting! You are stuck with me! I love you, you are my son, and this adoption is not going to fail."

He didn't answer immediately.

I waited for his response. I kept stroking his hair.

Finally, he said, from inside his sulk, "I hate that song. . . ."

"I'm sorry. I was desperate."

"It's child abuse," he grumbled.

"Hey, have a little pity on me. I had to *sing* it. I'll be a week getting it out of my head, and it'll probably take an industrial-strength dose of Gershwin to do it. Now, can you take the rest of your time-out without breaking any more holes in the wall?" No answer. "Let's try it."

Job had it easy. He only had boils, plague, rats, lice, stuff like that. I got whining, fussing, hateful stares, glowering, sulking, screaming, name-calling, rages, and shattered glass.

The house was broken, the dog was dead, I was too depressed to write (I couldn't write without a dog under the desk anyway), and I was afraid to ask, *what else could go wrong?*

Plenty. The devil child in the house north of us—one of a six-pack of sociopaths known around the neighborhood as "the Bundy Children"—falsely accused Dennis of acting out sexually with one of the little girls in the house south of us, and in the resultant feeding frenzy, I almost lost him.

A swarm of angry social workers swooped down out of the sky, broomsticks trailing ugly black smoke, and interviewed every kid within a six-block radius—there's nothing like a witch-hunt to traumatize a neighborhood. But this was something I *knew* Dennis hadn't done—it just wasn't part of his repertoire.

I did not have a chance to catch my breath.

Because one of the social workers had apparently discussed that piece of my private life she wasn't supposed to know, let alone discuss—shortly after that, the neighborhood Bundys, the ones who believed that a white-picket fence was sufficient evidence to demonstrate that they weren't intentionally malevolent, initiated a campaign of random acts of rudeness, vandalism, and abuse. The entire family, including the dog.*

There was no respite—

---

*This was eventually resolved by the state of California giving the number-three son 18–24 months of all-expense paid vacation, with time off for good behavior; which turned out to be all that the absentee father needed to sue for custody, thereby removing the remaining terrorist children from the neighborhood—and incidentally also alleviated me from the karmic burden of imagining acts of exquisite revenge. But for a while there . . .

THERE'S THIS THING ABOUT STORY-
telling—there are lots of things about storytelling, but there's
this one particular thing that I think is very interesting. I call
it the *flipover* scene. It almost always happens exactly halfway
through the story. I don't know why, but the rhythm of storytelling always seems to work that way.

In the flipover scene, the relationship changes between the
person and the problem. In the first half of the story, the problem works on the person; but the flipover scene is where the
person recognizes the essential nature of the problem—so in
the second half of the story, the person works on the problem.

What this means is that the second half of the story has a
different mood than the first half. It's always darker. Because
this is the part where the person is supposed to know what
he's doing and it still doesn't work—the situation gets worse.

I expect life to work this way. It doesn't, but that's the
expectation, because that's the way I structure the problems I
can solve. But stories are artificial, stories are *constructed*.
Stories happen because a storyteller picks and chooses what
parts he wants to put in. Just by stringing events together
that are otherwise unconnected, the storyteller assigns them
significance and gives them meaning. Only later do you look

at the artifice and see where the moment of realization occurred.

But when you're still living it, still in the middle, you don't know what's going to happen next—

~~~~~~~~~~~~~~~~~~~~~~~~

I HAVE THIS SERIES OF BOOKS I'VE written, about a starship called the *Star Wolf*. War in space, brave Earthmen fighting the evil Morthans. The *Star Wolf* is a battered little starship, trying to do its part in a much larger conflict. World War II in space. I was trying to turn it into a TV series.

We found some money for development—and paid for the construction of an elaborate starship model for a proof-of-concept video. The day the model builders delivered it, Dennis's eyes went wide with wonder.

The *Star Wolf* model was six feet long and four feet high. It had all the right details—insignia, serial numbers, emergency-access hatches, even running lights that actually worked. It had grappler spars for the stardrive, a bulge for the singularity containment, a docking bay underneath for the landing craft, missile housings, multiple plasma torches for subluminal vectoring, and even a two-man bubble-shaped observatory at the nose. The camera was going to love it.

"Is this your spaceship, Daddy?"

"Starship," I corrected. "Yes, it is. You mustn't touch it, sweetheart. It's very fragile and very expensive. It cost thousands and thousands of dollars. If this gets broken, there's no TV show. You must not touch this. Ever. Do you understand?"

"Uh-huh."

"I'm serious, Dennis. You cannot touch it. You cannot let your friends touch it. Don't even breathe near it. In fact, maybe we should both stop breathing for awhile."

Still looking at the model, Dennis asked softly, "Daddy?"

"What is it, sweetheart?"

"What can I be in the TV series?"

Uh-oh. "Um . . . well . . . You tell me. What would you like to be?"

"I could be this funny-looking guy who walks through the scene sometimes, only you never say who he is."

While one part of my mind was thinking of a polite way to say no, the *other* part of my mind was already visualizing it—like something out of David Lynch and *Mad* magazine. A four-foot-tall cockroach . . .

"I wouldn't have to say anything—" Dennis was already arguing. Negotiating. One step away from wheedling.

"You know," I said. "That's not a bad idea. It could work."

He hadn't heard me. "—I could have a mask that covers my face, so nobody would know it's me."

"Actually, that's a very good idea, Dennis. It's just what the show needs. Something different. Something that we never explain. Something for people to talk about and guess what it means—yeah, okay! You'll be the official Martian. And you'll walk through the background just once in every episode. And we'll never explain who you are. I like that. It's a wonderful idea. Thank you, Dennis." Within a week, I'd added Martian walk-throughs to the scripts for the first four episodes.

And now Dennis had an investment in our success. More important, he felt *included*.

But it didn't happen, because a few days later I came home from running errands, and the model was in pieces on the living room floor.

And no, we hadn't had another earthquake.

I felt as shattered as the starship. Everything we'd been working toward—

I lost it.

I finally lost it.

Big time.

Dadzilla.

Stomping through Northridge. Bellowing fire. Crushing cars. Knocking fighter planes from the sky.

Everything I'd been holding back. I finally let it out in one godawful, Earth-shattering roar.

Rationality disappeared. Rationality was impossible. Rationality was no longer operative in this continuum. Rationality was not a distinction in this paradigm. Rationality was meaningless. Rage, on the other hand—

It just hurt too much.

My life lay in pieces on the living-room floor.

And for the first time, I wondered if perhaps I'd made a huge mistake.

$\sim\sim\sim\sim\sim\sim\sim\sim\sim\sim\sim\sim\sim\sim$

WHEN THEY MAKE THE MOVIE OF this story—this is how they're going to play this conversation—they'll split me in two and let me argue with myself.

If the director is clever, he'll have one of me wearing the time travel belt—and maybe that godawful shirt as well.

I'll march into Dennis's room, I'll grab a suitcase. I'll start grabbing clothes in great handfuls, from the dresser drawers, from the closet—

—and then the other me will appear, standing in the closet door.

"You don't want to do this," he'll say. "Not really."

"You're right. I don't want to do this. I *have* to do this. For my own sanity. Get out of my way. I'm tired of arguing."

And then, Duplicate David—the voice of my sane self—will say what he always says: "You know, if you do this, you'll be just like everyone else in his life. Everyone who made promises they weren't going to keep, everyone who used him and used him up, everyone who betrayed him and abandoned him and turned him into what he is. But you're the only one who promised for keeps. So go ahead, prove to him that grown-ups can't be trusted. You're the last one."

And then, still angry, still stuffing clothes into the suit-case, I respond, "Guilt won't work on me! I have a Jewish mother. I've built up immunity." I stuff some more clothes into the suitcase. I'm not even looking any more. "You're so stupid. For a figment of my imagination, you're a real disappointment. Is that the best you can do? Guilt?"

"You can do better?"

"Of course, I can. Why didn't you talk about commitment? And making a difference? About hitting the wall—and breaking through instead of just breaking down. About not being a quitter. I mean, your crappy argument is just more evidence that I can't handle this, and never will."

I find my rhythm now. I keep going. "You should be telling me that being a dad isn't just something you do. It's who you are. A kid isn't a trophy or a fashion accessory. And you don't just give up because you get your silly plastic spaceship broken. You're in it for the duration.

"Being a dad—it's a promise. And you have to keep it because you love your kid, no matter what. He's your favorite kid in the whole world, and you'd do anything for him. You'd die without him. And it doesn't matter that he's a Martian or anything else. *He's still my kid. And I love him—*"

I stop. I look at the duplicate of myself. "There. That's the argument you should have used!"

"Yep. That's the argument I should have used. Next time, I will."

"You son of a bitch! There isn't going to be a next time."

It will be a great scene. The audience will love it. And I'll put the clothes back on the hangers, back in the closet, back in the dresser drawers.

And that will look like the moment of transformation. That moment when the hero realizes who he is.

But it isn't.

It wasn't.

It is never really that easy.

I'll explain . . .

~~~~~~~~~~~~~~~~~~~~

S EE—

I tell stories.

About everything.

There's Chuck, the bad-luck fairy. The one who walked through my life and cost me a job, two friendships, my self-esteem, and caused my favorite Japanese restaurant to burn down. There's Ghu, the cosmic badger, the god who lives in the ceiling, the one who looks back when you look up, and who doesn't give a rat's rectum about what humans want, doesn't want to be worshiped, and gets really annoyed whenever anyone invokes his name. And then there's that freezer full of rat rectums that *nobody* has given—and if somebody doesn't start giving rat rectums soon I'm going to have to make chili again. And don't forget pickled mongoose either.

It's *all* stories.

The job of the storyteller is to get lost in the story. He has to tell it as if it's real. And that means getting inside it and living it and forgetting that it's only a story. You have to tell it like you're reporting it, not making it up.

What that means—

—is that the people I make up are more real than the people I live with.

The kid in the story isn't the kid in my lap. And the difference—

Oh, hell.

Confession time.

—I know how it happened. When and where it happened. The price I paid. And why I paid it. *The decision I made.*

It happened in another lifetime.

When I was young and stupid. Not yet a person.

His name was Steve.

He had red hair and green eyes. He smiled back at me. And that's how it started. We smiled. And then we talked. We sat and talked for hours. It didn't matter what we talked about—we were fascinated by each other.

And when finally, we fell inevitably into bed, *something happened*—something that went beyond trust and intimacy and sharing. We came out somewhere else—*connected.* We became a place where self has neither boundaries nor conditions. Mutual recognition existed in the moments we created. I hadn't know it was possible; neither had he. We fell into each other and celebrated the sharing.

Steve was joyous. And because he was joyous, he was beautiful. Steve was generous. And because he was generous, he was astonishing.

We fell in love.

I'd never felt anything like it before—it transcended my experience. It ripped me open like I was giving birth to myself.

I was no longer me, but part of something so much larger, I couldn't comprehend it all—a profound connection that left us both breathless, crying, and choked up in wonder. I saw God in the face of my lover. We cried for happiness in each other's arms, and after that I was never the same again, because no matter what else happened in my life, I knew I was loved. For a very short time—for one magical summer, when all the days were golden—I knew what it was to be happy.

And then summer ended with a gunshot in the face. And Steve was gone. In a crime so horrible that people still talk about it. I read the news today, oh boy . . .

And when the shock wore off, as the realization sank in, as the present slid horribly into the past, I went crazy.

I'd been given the gift of knowledge, a glimpse of what was possible. And then it had been snatched away. Now that I knew what I didn't have, life was about what I'd lost.

I wasn't a nice person to be around. Not for a long time. Desperate. Anxious. Scared. Bitter. I felt cheated. I struck out at others. I was hurtful.

And I really couldn't talk to anybody about it. Because

there wasn't anyone I trusted enough. I didn't know anyone who might even come close to understanding. So I held it close to me, like a wound I was hiding, and staggered on, waving away all others, because I knew they couldn't help—not unless they knew how to bring Steve back.

I should have just hung a warning sign on myself: *Beware of toxic jerk.* I said stupid things to a lot of people. I didn't care.

I used my writing as a retreat, in both senses of the word. A withdrawal from defeat. A safe haven.

I was writing a novel, my first one—about a sentient computer, an intelligence engine named HARLIE.

One day, HARLIE wakes up and asks, WHAT DOES IT MEAN TO BE A HUMAN BEING? And the chief of the project has to sit down at the keyboard and try to figure out how to answer the question—a question he'd never even asked himself.

And then the computer asks, WHAT IS LOVE? (In those days, computers talked in all caps.)

There's this thing that writers talk about—where the characters take on a life of their own and they run away with the story, taking it off to places the author never intended to go. That's what happened here.

Except, that's not what really happens. That's one of the stories that writers tell about storytelling.

What really happened was that I sat and wrote and had a conversation with myself—a conversation that wasn't possible, unless I let part of myself pretend it was someone else—a disembodied voice in the typewriter. And so I typed. I typed everything I felt and feared and worried about, everything I thought I knew, and everything else as well, the much larger domain of what I didn't know and didn't know how to figure out.

Because this, at last, was a place where I could talk to somebody about it all—and if that somebody was really me, that was okay too, because I was the guy who had to figure it out anyway. So I had all these conversations with myself—and the different parts of me talked into the keyboard. And talked and talked and talked.

And then, one day, I figured something out. It wasn't perfect, but it was a start.

See—it was about Steve's legacy. He died before he had a chance to make a difference. If I let his death ruin my life, then the only difference he'd made was negative. But I still had my memories of how good we were together, and if I concentrated on what he'd given me in our own private summer of love, and if I *chose* to become a better person as a way of keeping him with me, then his legacy would be positive, and that would be the gift I could give to him.

And yes, I knew that was just another story that I was making up, something else that I was adding to a random act of violence. But so what? At least this was a better story to live than the other one. And if I didn't have the knowledge that I was loved, then at least I could take comfort in the knowledge that I *could* be loved. And that was a good place to begin.

And when the book about HARLIE was finished, it was a love story. About people falling in love and discovering their own humanity.

So, that's what I did for twenty years. I wrote about humanity. I wrote about love. I could live inside my stories very comfortably. It was safe to live there, because I was in control.

But all that writing about love wasn't the same as *actually* loving.

And when I finally figured it out—or at least got the first inkling that I was metaphorically playing with myself—that's when I applied to adopt a little boy.

Because.

After everything else—

—it wasn't just about knowing I could be loved. That was only half of the equation. The other half was that—

I could create love.

~~~~~~~~~~~~~~~~~~~~~~

I SIT DOWN AT THE KEYBOARD. I TYPE: HARLIE?

And the other half of myself replies: HELLO, BOSS. IT'S BEEN A LONG TIME. <LOOKS AROUND> HM, NOT BAD. I LIKE THIS NEW PLACE.

Want to talk?

OF COURSE. I'M HERE ALL THE TIME, YOU KNOW THAT.

I want to talk about Dennis.

NO, YOU DON'T.

Oh? Then who do I want to talk about?

YOURSELF.

Moi?

OUI, VOUS. WHENEVER YOU SIT DOWN AT THE KEYBOARD, IT'S ALWAYS ABOUT YOU. YOU THINK I DON'T NOTICE? YOU'RE VERY SELF-INDULGENT.

Yeah. But at least I do it with style.

IF YOU SAY SO.

I say so. Allow me one illusion.

WITH YOU, IT'S ALL ILLUSION. EVEN I AM AN ILLUSION.

But a useful one, you have to admit.

WHAT'S THE PROBLEM?

The story.

WHICH STORY?

The story about how much I love him. I made it up that if I loved him enough, that if I did enough, that if I gave him enough of everything, that it would make a difference, that he would turn into a real boy.

HE IS A REAL BOY.

I know that. He is what he is.

BUT HE DOESN'T FIT YOUR PICTURES OF WHAT YOU THINK HE SHOULD BE.

Yes. That's the problem. I have a story. And the facts don't match.

YOU DON'T HAVE A STORY.

I don't?

WHAT YOU HAVE IS YOUR EGO IN DISGUISE.

sigh Okay. Yes. I have ego on my face. I admit it.

WHY DID YOU ADOPT HIM?

I've been wondering about that myself.

SO WHY DID YOU ADOPT HIM?

Remember, that was the one question that I couldn't answer. I faked it. I said I wanted to be someone's dad. I didn't know what else to write.

SO ANSWER THE QUESTION NOW. WHY DID YOU ADOPT HIM?

Because. I had to.

WHY?

I stared at the screen in frustration. I hate that word. "Why" is the word that lets people tell stories instead of what's so. Pushed back. Made a face. Pulled forward, put my hands back on the keyboard—

WHY?

Because—I was a Martian child too.

Because way back when I was a kid, when I was the smallest and the smartest, when I was getting picked on every day, when I was teased just for being alive, I knew that someday the Martians would come and get me. There would be a ship—not a rocket ship, but something else, something that glowed and sparkled—and it would be at night, out in a great, grassy field—and it would come down and open up for me, all golden inside, and the people would recognize me as one of their own, and they would welcome me aboard, and I would be safe, I would be home where I belonged, where people like me loved each other and took care of each other—and we would sail off into the sky and away to the stars. And we would never hurt again, we would never be lonely again.

But they never came. It never happened.

NEVER?

I grew up. The Martians, or whoever they were, they never arrived. Maybe they didn't care enough. Maybe they didn't know where I was. Maybe they didn't know who I was. And maybe I wasn't good enough. I can't tell you how much that hurt. And then . . . finally, one day I realized that I was on my own. So I made it up that it was just a childhood fantasy, a little daydream. A place to hide out. And eventually, I forgot about it. At least, I thought I'd forgotten. But when I heard about Dennis, I knew he was me—who I used to be. And I knew that the Martians weren't going to come for him, either. But I could. I could be there for him. So he wouldn't have to be alone. Like I was. So, I didn't have a choice. I *had* to adopt him.

THAT'S NOT ALL OF IT, DAVID.

It isn't?

WHAT DID *YOU* WANT TO GET?

. . . That was the question I couldn't answer on the motivational questionnaire. Why do you want to adopt a child? I couldn't answer it because I didn't know—like a caterpillar spinning a cocoon, he doesn't know why he has to, he just has to do it. It's what comes next. I didn't know what I would get because I didn't know what there was to get. Nobody knows what it means to be a mom or a dad until after they've become a mom or a dad and lived it for a while.

But this is what it is—you get a kid in your life, you give up sleep, you give up privacy, you give up freedom. You give up yourself. But you don't mind, because there's this incredible joy in living for someone else, in the adventure of watching that person *become*.

But if you ask me that question now, I know the answer. It's obvious. It's been obvious all along.

What you get is this thing called *family*. A place to belong. A place to be who you are. That's what you get. *Yourself*.

And that's really all that you ever want.

Yeah.

~~~~~~~~~~~~~~~~~~~~~~~~

O<small>KAY, SO HERE'S HOW IT RESOLVES</small>— here's the only way it can resolve. There isn't any way to stop telling stories. Storytelling is the fundamental act of communication. It's a major part of being human.

Every time a person communicates, he tells a little

story—what happened to the last piece of chocolate cake, why the dog is wearing your sister's hat, and why the UFO's haven't returned Elvis yet. Big stories, little stories. Why I was late for work, why I was speeding, and how this phone number got into my wallet. I can explain everything. *I can tell a story.*

The stories we tell—that's us explaining how we think the world works. Once we speak it, once we say it aloud, that makes it *real* for us—and real for everyone else who hears it too. When we tell a story, we invite people to visit our reality. We invite them to move in. Our stories are the reality we live in.

That's very powerful.

Because we can *choose* what stories we want to tell—we can choose the stories we want to *live.*

Here's my story—

~~~~~~~~~~~~~~~~~~~~~~~~~~

THE MARTIANS
or whoever they were
took me inside.

And we had a conversation, except it wasn't a conversation—not the way human beings have conversations. What human beings call communication is really just a chaotic game of Russian telephone. It's a triumph of commitment over confusion that any of us ever really think we understand anything that anyone else says.

Martians don't do that.

What Martians do is *something else*. And I can't explain it because what Martians do occurs outside of the domain of language.

Oh. And they weren't Martians. They were *something else*.

What it *was*—

—*there aren't any Martians.*

We are the Martians.

Except we don't know it.

When we had ourselves born as human beings, we forgot we were also Martians.

Except, sometimes, some of us remember for a while. We remember only until we get swamped by human language and human storytelling, which so overwhelms Martian thinking with its own peculiar logic that it makes Martian thinking impossible.

Most of us forget we're Martians as fast as we're infected with language—but sometimes, some of us don't get caught up in language as fast as everyone else, so for a while . . . we're something else.

Dennis didn't get languaged on schedule because he didn't have anyone committed to languaging him. I didn't—because I didn't. Not until I was three and a half did I start talking. My parents worried that I might be slow. I made up for it later.

But there isn't any us-and-them. There's only us. And

*when we talk about us and them, we're actually telling our-
selves a lie about us.*

We are the Martians.

And that's why I'm raising a Martian.

Because I'm the Martian dad.

And that's why it all happened.

Not because he created it, but because I did.

~~~~~~~~~~~~~~~~~~~~~~~~~~~~~~

AND THAT'S THE POINT.

He's not the Martian Child.

I am.

I made it up.

And now I have to unmake it.

~~~~~~~~~~~~~~~~~~~~~~~~~~~~~~

MY MISTAKE—AND IT WAS THE
worst one I could have made—was that I had forgotten my
priorities. I was worrying about myself and not about him.

I'd forgotten the basics. Human beings never really solve

problems, we just remodel them. While I was figuring out how to handle an eight-year-old, he'd turned into a ten-year-old. While I was working on giving him a safe place to grow, he was already packing to move on.

Dennis had never stayed anywhere longer than two years—so he had it wired up that nothing was permanent; everything ended after two years. He knew that one day, Kathy Bright would arrive and have one of *those* conversations. "Dennis, we've found a new place for you to live. They're very nice people, you're going to like living with them—" He knew this was the way it worked, because that's what always happened. That's what had happened everywhere else.

That was why things were heading downhill. Because in Dennis's mind, this was over—this didn't matter anymore. If he wasn't staying, why behave? Why care about *anything?*

I had read about this phenomenon—it was in the books and on the tapes about adopting an older kid. This is how these kids think. What's the difference between an adoptive home and a foster home? Nothing, really—you still have a caseworker checking in once a month. The concept of permanence doesn't exist in that paradigm.

Somewhere in there—perhaps when Somewhere died—Dennis began packing his emotional suitcase. In his world, he was already sitting on the front porch, waiting for Kathy to arrive.

So when I went to his room to have a conversation with my invisible self and pack his ugly old suitcase, the one he wouldn't let me throw out—it wasn't there.

He'd already packed it himself. He'd left most of the clothes I'd bought for him, he'd taken his T-shirt signed by Wayne Gretzky and his ragged old stuffed gingerbread man and the big blue bunny, but not much else. I couldn't be sure. At the rate things were lost and broken around here, I couldn't tell what was missing. Oh, his little folder of photos, the only record he had of his past.

He'd broken the starship model.

And he'd panicked.

He'd grabbed the few things he couldn't live without. And he'd run away.

But where would he go? Where *could* he go?

The Johnson group home had closed its doors a year ago, parceling out the various children to new placements. He couldn't go there. He wouldn't have gone to any of his friends.

He used to talk about New Mexico—somebody he knew and liked had moved there once. No, I didn't think he was on his way to New Mexico—

And then I remembered.

It was a long shot.

One night, I'd tucked him into bed. He was lying there, watching me, and I was sitting next to him, looking at him, stroking his hair, just talking, not about anything in particular—I asked him to remember something good. We'd been together long enough that we had memories to share now—but instead of getting happy, he got sad.

"What's the matter, sweetheart?"

"I'm going to miss you."

"I'm not going anywhere."

"No. I am."

"You are? Where?"

"I have to go back to Mars."

"Not any time soon, I hope."

He didn't answer.

Suddenly, he grabbed me hard around the neck and hugged me tightly—as if he were leaving tonight. "I love you, Daddy."

"I love you too, sweetheart. You're my favorite kid in the whole world."

His little body was stiff with tension. This was a hug of desperation. After a bit, I held him at arm's length and looked into his eyes. "You know, you don't have to go if you don't want to. You can stay here with me as long as you want."

"I can't. I have to go."

"When?"

"When they come."

"It's a long trip. Should I pack you a sandwich?"

"No, I'll eat when I get there."

"That's good. Do they have pickled mongoose?"

"Nuh-uh."

"Do they have peanut butter and jellyfish?"

"Nuh-uh."

"Can I meet them? Will they stay for dinner? Do they like spaghetti?"

"Nuh-uh."

"Why not?"

"They won't come here."

"Oh? Where are they coming to? Do you want me to drive you?"

"No. I'll walk."

"To where?"

"To the park."

"Why the park?"

"Because that's where they'll come."

"Oh, that makes sense, I guess."

"Uh-huh."

"When are they coming?"

"They come at nighttime. So nobody will see them."

"Oh. Well, if it's too late at night, I'll have to walk you over there. So, you'll let me know when. Okay?"

He didn't answer.

"Listen. If you decide you want to stay, I can talk to them. I'll tell them it's all right with me if it's all right with them. Okay?"

"They won't talk to you."

"They won't?"

"Nuh-uh."

Of course not. I was *human*. And he was Martian. That was the story we were living in. Martians don't *talk* to humans. Not in language anyway.

"Are you going to have a window seat?"

"Uh-huh."

"That's good. I think you'd better go to sleep now, or

you'll be too tired to go to Mars." I tucked the bunny under his arm again. "Is the bunny going too?"

"Uh-huh."

"Good. Otherwise he'll get lonely."

I pulled his blanket up and kissed him good night again. "I love you, Martian child."

He didn't answer.

~~ ~~ ~~ ~~ ~~ ~~ ~~ ~~ ~~ ~~ ~~ ~~ ~~ ~~

It was a long shot, but . . .

I grabbed some things and drove over to the park.

It was another one of those dry, windy nights that defy description. The air is restless and the trees start whispering secrets to each other. A discomforting reminder of the desert that sprawled here before the city was built—it makes the world ephemeral and temporary, as if by morning all this will be dust again.

The park was an artificial oasis in the night—bright and empty, nascent with brooding possibility. As if something large was breathing in the outer darkness.

I found Dennis sitting on a stone bench, alone in a pool of illumination, surrounded by the waiting unknown. His suitcase was beside him. A cosmic bus stop. He looked very small.

He did not look up as I approached.

I sat down next to him.

I waited, but he didn't speak.

"You forgot your jacket—" I passed it across to him. He didn't put it on. He laid it carefully on the bench.

"So tonight's the night, huh?"

"Uh-huh."

"Will you phone me when you get there? So I know you got there safely?"

"I don't think they have a telephone."

"Oh. Well, then maybe you could write me a letter? Here, you can take my favorite pen."

He took it and put it in his pocket.

"Did you remember to pack clean underwear?"

"Da-ad . . ." Two syllables. Impatience. Don't push it.

"I just don't want them to think I didn't take good care of you. I'd get in a lot of trouble, wouldn't I? I mean, if the Martians thought I hadn't taken good care of you, I could get disneygraded, couldn't I?"

"You're not going to get disneygraded."

"I'm not?"

"I told them not to. You were nice to me. Mostly."

"Oh, good. Thank you. I was worried about that."

"Try not to be too sad, okay?"

"Okay."

We sat in silence for a while. I looked up at the sky. You can't really see stars anywhere near Los Angeles. Too much haze in the air, too much light coming off the smoldering city.

But tonight . . . there were stars. Not a lot, but some. But no Martian UFO.

I fumbled around in my pocket. "Oh, here. You forgot your toothbrush. You'll need that too." I passed it over.

He took it and laid it on top of the jacket.

"Well, I guess this is it." I stood up as if to go. He didn't look like he wanted to be hugged. I held out my hand—

Abruptly, belligerently, the words came pouring out of him. "I broke the model! I screwed up everything! I'm not good enough for you! You don't want a Martian for a son!"

"Yes, I do!" I blurted it out too fast to think about it. "I don't care what planet you're from. I don't want you to go! I love you more than anyone in the world. You're the son I always wanted. And I want to be the dad you wished for."

He looked at me, eyes wide. Startled. I'd said this to him a thousand times before, but tonight was the first time he'd heard it.

Dennis sniffed once. Not a wet sniff, just an uncertain little intake of breath, as if caught off guard.

He rubbed at his nose, and when he looked up again, he was wearing his *let's-get-serious* face.

I sat back down on the bench and waited. He had to preamble for a while, then he'd amble for a while, and finally, after he'd worked on it for a bit, then he'd segue into whatever it was he really wanted to say. I waited while he assembled the cars of his train of thought.

"Daddy?"

"Yes, sweetheart."

"I have to tell you something."

"Okay."

"I don't think you want to hear it."

"Yes, I do."

"I don't want you to get mad."

"I won't get mad. I promise."

"You promise?"

"I promise."

"Pinky promise?"

"Absolutely pinky promise."

"I don't know how to say this."

"Just say it."

"You won't get mad?

"Go ahead, Dennis, you can tell me."

He looked into my eyes, searching my feelings. Finally, he said, "I don't want to be a Martian anymore."

It was like that moment in the meeting—when I started looking for a folder labeled *Martian*. I heard the words, but not the meaning. And then, even after I did hear the meaning, I still didn't realize what he meant.

Was he saying he didn't want to play the Martian game anymore? Or was he telling me something deeper? The serious look on his face showed that this was something very important to him.

I didn't know what to say.

The last time I didn't know what to say, he'd been bawling about a blanket. And all I could do was echo his words back to him. It had worked then—

So I said, "You don't want to be a Martian anymore."

"Nuh-uh."

"Okay," I agreed.

It was that easy.

He relaxed.

And then he said, "I just want a daddy."

I was suddenly having trouble catching my breath.

—the look on his face, I'd never seen him so real before—

And then I finally found the right words. It was so silly, I had to say it. "Is that a Martian wish?" I asked.

He nodded, somberly. "Yes." He must have known what he was giving up.

For a moment . . . it felt as if reality was flickering.

Maybe it was just me. Maybe it was just my overactive imagination. Maybe it was the power of suggestion. And maybe it was just that we were creating a new agreement between the two of us and the universe was agreeing too.

But, something shifted—

In front of me was a small, frightened little boy, with very big eyes, and an expression that could break your heart. I reached out and put my hands on his shoulders and looked at him for a long moment. "I think it worked."

"I think so too."

"Well, good—" But the moment wasn't finished, wasn't quite complete. "Now it's my turn to make a wish." I whispered very softly, "Do you know what I'm wishing for?"

He started to shake his head. Then he stopped and

looked at me. And he got it. He flung himself onto me and wrapped his arms around me and held on as tightly as he could.

He held on forever.

Martians aren't the only ones who can wish.

~~~~~~~~~~~~~~~~~~~~~~~~~~~~

W E WALKED OUT OF THE PARK together. He didn't look back. I snuck a peek, just in case.

But, no—

They never did come.

Afterword

~~~~~~

*D*ENNIS'S ADOPTION WAS FINALIZED ON MARCH 3, 1995. *As part of the adoption, he changed his name to Sean.*

At the time of this writing, he is seventeen years old. He's weathered the usual storms of adolescence without too much damage to his father's sanity and shows dangerous signs of maturity and responsibility.

He is no longer a Martian. He no longer makes stoplights change, he doesn't identify the color of M&M's by how they taste, and he has not been able to wish the Dodgers into the World Series. Nor have we won the lotto.

There are lots of nice things in the world to wish for, but it's more fun making them happen the old-fashioned way.